Beyond the Misty Fells

Gill Frances: Content Editor

Anna Nolan: Copy Editor, Typesetter and Publisher

Skiddaw Writers

Ann Bowker
Rowland Bowker
Victoria Bowmer
Gill Frances
Jean Gallagher
Aline Hopkins
John Howell
Christine Mitchell
Anna Nolan

ISBN   978 – 1 – 326 – 39144 – 7

E-book is also available

Contents

Introduction

In this unusual collection of travellers' tales, nine Lake District authors invite you to share their journeys in time and space. Open these pages, and you will bounce across Botswana on safari, discover a 'lost' photographer in Chicago, spin prayer-wheels in India, touch a famously hot rock, take pleasure in a very special flight over Taranaki and endure jetlag in Canberra.

Closer to home, you can join a woman on an amazing trek across Wales and another on a bike ride to the pub . . . And whereas Lyme Regis presents a disconcerting challenge to one holiday-maker, a fish proves to be more of a problem for another.

Perhaps the quirkiest pieces in the collection are those which tempt you to explore a very different landscape, or should we say 'mindscape': nothing less than the English language itself, with its booby-traps for the unwary user who loses the path in the middle of a sentence, dangles participles over the abyss of misunderstanding and risks doing away with granny for lack of punctuation.

On a serious note, one author finds out what really happened to her father in the Second World War, whilst a second looks back on two 'mercy' missions – one to Romania and one to Jordan. Folk who are interested in Fair Trade will be fascinated by the 'inside story' of the connection between Keswick and Ethiopia.

So join Skiddaw Writers as they leave their own magical, misty fells behind and explore the worlds which lie beyond.

Acknowledgements

This is a collection of writings published by the Skiddaw U3A Creative Writing Group. Currently, the Convenor of the group is Gill Frances. Details of how to join Skiddaw U3A are available on the website at: www.skiddawu3a.co.uk and in local publications.

Gill would like to thank all members of the group for the fascinating discussions and endless fun over the last year and a half. The writing has been pretty good, too.

The whole group wishes to express its appreciation of, and gratitude for, the beautiful cover photograph, supplied by Aline Hopkins.

Ann Bowker, Rowland Bowker, Victoria Bowmer, Gill Frances, Jean Gallagher, Aline Hopkins, John Howell and Christine Mitchell would also like to give sincere and very special thanks to one of our number, namely our chief copy editor, Anna Nolan. Without her expertise, patience and hard work, our journey would not have had a happy ending. Thank you, Anna.

About Skiddaw Writers

Ann Bowker

Ann has always been a keen walker and peak bagger. She has climbed most of the Marilyns (hills with a 150 metre drop all round). Only five hills on St Kilda remain unclimbed, two of them sea stacks.

Rowland Bowker

Rowland was born in Cheshire. He says that his father, who ran a poultry farm and had no opportunity to travel himself, was always talking about going to faraway places and read only books on travel. When Rowland was eight years old, he received from his father the gift of an atlas. It was a gift that was to influence him for the rest of his life.

Victoria Bowmer

Victoria is a traveller who enjoys the journey as much as the destination. While being a lover of nature and the great outdoors, she also appreciates cities with interesting stories to tell, having visited the churches of Rome, the art galleries of Madrid and the shiny cobbled streets of Dubrovnik to name but a few.

Gill Frances

Gill comes from South Wales and has taught English for many years. Her retirement plans did not include dodgy knees or quite so many grandchildren. The U3A has been a joyful discovery – so many things to learn and so many lovely and talented people to learn them with. (That's a preposition at the end of a sentence, but she does not love grammar quite as much as Anna does.)

Jean Gallagher

Jean was born and brought up in Sunderland. Educated at the Bede School, she became a primary teacher. Married with three children, she taught in various locations until retirement. After divorce in 1989, she became a successful businesswoman. She has always enjoyed writing stories, and this is her third book.

Aline Hopkins

Aline was born in Sheffield but now lives in the Lake District, her ancestral home. One day she intends to find out if any of her Elliott ancestors were Border Reivers. Since the 1980s, she has occasionally written for various publications, including magazines, newspapers, journals and newsletters. Her main passions at the moment are travel and photography (and a bit of writing).

John Howell

John was born in Hyde, Cheshire, and has practised and taught chemical engineering in four continents. On retiring from the University of Bath in 2002, he moved to the Lakes with the determination to do something completely different. He has repaired fell footpaths, organised a Rotary micro-loan project in Ethiopia and tried his hand at creative writing.

Christine Mitchell

Christine followed her job around Britain whilst travelling around the world on vacation. A fell-walker in her younger days, she retired to the Lake District, which she had first seen as a teenager and had visited many times since. She also decided to take up new interests: first, art and then history, archaeology and creative writing.

Anna Nolan

Having contentedly resided in Britain since 1981, Anna is a Polish linguist/ grammarian, educationalist, writer and editor with a penchant for irreverent satire. The English language being her all-consuming passion, she pens books, articles and blog posts on English grammar, punctuation and usage, trying to do so in a jocular way whenever appropriate. Her website/ blog can be found at: http://flaming-english.com/.

1

The journey into the rest of my life

by Aline Hopkins

"I can't die yet, I haven't seen Ayers Rock," I said to God and anyone else with a say in the matter. This was one of the first things going through my mind when I woke up in the intensive care unit of a Yorkshire hospital after a serious road accident. I'd had other brief moments of lucidity, but the overwhelming pain from every cell in my body soon sent me back into unconsciousness. One unfortunate awakening occurred just as a doctor was pushing a tube through my ribcage into my collapsed left lung. I've never possessed good timing.

This was my wake-up call, a sudden realisation that I might not have survived and that the things which were important to me, such as seeing Ayers Rock, couldn't be put off. I'd spent far too much of my time and energy on an organisation which couldn't care less about me, when I should have been putting my energies into myself, and the things I wanted to do.

During the weeks in hospital, I had plenty of time to put together a list of all the things I wanted to see and do. These days, this is popularly known as a 'bucket' list, but I prefer to think of it as my 'do-it-while-you-can' list. Ayers Rock was in first place. It was about two years later, after many months on crutches and lots of physiotherapy, that I decided I should go to Australia to see this monolith which had called to me from the other side of the world.

Beyond the Misty Fells

I flew via Singapore, a notably unmemorable flight except for the large man sitting to my right who kept lifting the seat arm so he could expand into my space. At every opportunity, I would put the arm down, and, at every opportunity, he would raise it again. Changi Airport gave an hour's respite, and I was pleased to see he was not sitting next to me on the next leg of the trip, to Sydney. After a fitful few hours' sleep in Sydney, I was back at the airport boarding a flight to Alice Springs. Walking from the plane to the small terminal building after arrival, I learned the true meaning of 'prickly heat'. It must have been over 40 degrees, and the heat felt like thousands of small pins prickling against my skin.

A flight to Ayers Rock, or Uluru, as it is known to the Aborigines and is now more correctly called, followed. The pilot almost immediately informed the passengers that it was going to be a bumpy ride because of the hot air rising up from the desert below. A switchback ride at a fairground couldn't have had more ups and downs, and I'm sorry to admit that some days later I chickened out of taking the flight back and went by bus instead.

The airport at Uluru was small but lined with kiosks selling various trips to, up and around the Rock. I booked on three straightaway. My first view of the Rock made me think of a pink marshmallow floating in a red mist; it rises so markedly from the flat red sands around it. A red cherry on a bun with pink icing. I must have been hungry. After settling in at the hotel, I went on my first excursion to the Rock. I marvelled at it all the way and felt a strong sense of it calling. After all I had been through, here I was, and there it was.

I walked up to it and placed my hand upon it. It was hot. A hot rock. I guess I was expecting some sort of spiritual experience, a connection, some kind of feeling. In a way, I felt disappointed, but even

2

though I had been through hell, I was half-way round the world standing next to one of its most amazing natural wonders.

It was a start. It is still my reminder that life can be short. It can't be taken for granted that you can do things 'later'. Since then, I have ticked many things off my list – Italy, Yellowstone, the Taj Mahal, the Aurora Borealis, learning Spanish, and have been around the world twice.

I still have that original list, but I also have an ongoing list, which I add to occasionally as I cross things off. I haven't been hot-air ballooning yet, or seen Victoria Falls, or visited Angkor Wat, or been to Wimbledon, but they're on the list.

One of these days, I'm going to go back to Uluru, and I will go up to the Rock, put my hand on it and say, very quietly, "Thank you".

But not yet.

2

The one that didn't get away

by Victoria Bowmer

What comes to mind when you think of Scotland? For me, it's majestic mountains, craggy cliffs, tumbling streams, wild moorland and glassy lochs. Today sees Scotland at its best; indeed, Sunday mornings anywhere don't come much better than this. The country has belied its reputation for wet and windy weather, so I am performing a slow striptease in tandem with the rising sun's increasing heat. Firstly, I lose my fleece, then my jumper, and now I am down to a tee-shirt. It's a joy to discover that the voracious midges Scotland is famous for have decamped elsewhere, so I can enjoy the warm breeze on my arms without the prospect of an evening dabbing calamine lotion onto itchy spots.

Today's adventure began when I saw an advertisement at a hotel reception for fly fishing tuition with a local gillie. Having walked along many a canal bank without understanding why anybody would want to sit for hours staring at a rod dangling in muddy water, I have secretly been attracted to the glamour of standing in a river, waders up to my thighs, elegantly casting a delicate fly to outwit a canny wild salmon. It may have started in the dim and distant past with a newspaper photograph of Princess Diana sitting by a river gazing lovingly at Prince Charles as he fished during their Scottish honeymoon. How could she not have wanted to be in the river with him?

Beyond the Misty Fells

So today finds me standing in a loch-side field with my eyes being drawn not towards the magnificent mountains or gleaming water but to the unfeasibly long, slim and, I am guessing, very bendy fishing rod lying on the grass in front of me. I have the concentration span of a Scottish midge so am relieved when, after a frustrating half hour standing listening about the reel, line and fly, I am at last allowed to pick up the precious rod. It seems the local trout may have nothing to worry about, as my early casting efforts catch a plastic chair, a bush and my rucksack, all of which are behind me. Perhaps I could try a new style of backwards fishing?

With a little perseverance from me and endless patience from the gillie, everything suddenly clicks. The secret is not to rush but to get into a rhythm. To resist the urge to flick the rod in a kinky whip action and to cheat a little by pushing the end of the handle up my sleeve. Realising that the worst I can do is tangle the line or lose the fly, I begin to relax. Arm up, pause, arm down, watch the fly start to sink, pause, pull in some line, and so it goes on. As time passes, it becomes automatic, like driving a car and not remembering the journey, and I have time to breathe in the sweet air, hear the silence and appreciate my surroundings.

As I was to discover, fly fishing is long periods of calm during which a Zen-like peace takes over, interspersed with moments of frantic activity. I was awoken from my trance by a gentle but definite tug on my line. Having completely forgotten what to do in the unlikely event of getting a bite, I embarrassingly squealed for help. My gillie, jolted out of his own reverie, meandered over and gently held the rod with me. I think we repeatedly let the line slacken, then drew it in again until the fish was close to the bank. I am not exactly sure because I was so stunned to have had a bite, and mesmerised by the flashes of silver scales as the fish grew gradually closer, that it was all a daze.

That afternoon, walking back up the hill to my accommodation gently swinging an old carrier bag weighed down with a trout which would, that evening, feed four of us with enough left for seconds, I felt very different from the person who had walked down the hill that morning.

Learning a new skill is supposedly good for both the brain and the soul, so, along with vitamin D from the day's sun and the fatty acids from the fish I would be eating later, I should be ending the day a happier and healthier person than the one who woke up this morning. I find myself wondering if anyone has written a book *Zen and the Art of Fly Fishing*. Since returning home, I have been online and checked, and, yes, they have.

3

Across the dragon's back

by Ann Bowker

In 1993, Ann Bowker celebrated her retirement by walking across Wales from south to north. The walk included the tops of all 181 Welsh 'two thousanders' (that is, mountains of 2,000 feet or over) and covered 500 miles. Ann completed the five-week walk on schedule without ever accepting a lift. Along the way, she often camped and sometimes stayed in B&Bs or, occasionally and more luxuriously, hotels. What follows are extracts from her book, *Across the Dragon's Back: One Woman's Walk over the Welsh Mountains*.

7th April

It is always a strange feeling, when the tent is packed away, to turn and leave the camping spot, which now looks like any other bit of hillside. This morning, my presence could have been detected by a dry patch, but not for long. There was thick mist and a persistent drizzle. I contoured round Foel Fraith, which is less than 2000 feet high and which has a very stony top, as I had observed last night. I was navigating by compass and estimating, as I turned around the hill, the place to drop down to the col, so was pleased to have my estimate confirmed by the sight of the rising slopes of Garreg Las ahead. This hill is also very stony, and it was impossible to avoid entirely the slippery boulder fields on its rather flat top. I knew that the summit is crowned by two large and ancient cairns, which I had seen from Garreg Lwyd, so there was no danger of missing the top in the mist.

As would happen many times, I now joined a segment of one of the routes described in the Nuttalls' book.[1] This time, I was following it in reverse. The Nuttalls had mentioned a large cairn on the grassy summit of Waun Lefrith, but I never found it. Fortunately, this top has too little re-ascent to count as a separate mountain in their list, so, as soon as I reached the unmistakeable edge of the escarpment, I simply turned right and followed it to the top of Picws Du. I met a couple coming down from this summit – the only other people I met on these hills. What a pity it was to be traversing this splendid ridge on such a dismal day. The cliffs sweep down to the corrie lake Llyn y Fan Fach and round northwards to the bold prow which makes this hill so easy to pick out in distant views. Today, the drama was only in the mind, the picture of cliff and lake and sky and brilliant sunshine half-remembered from a visit long ago.

Yet there is pleasure in walking in the mist. Walker and hill are enfolded together in a dank, grey intimacy. On a day of sharpness and clarity, the eye and the heart are drawn to the distant horizon, the arching sky and the sweeping ridge. Today, every rock and every tussock, every little twist in the line of the escarpment is, for one moment, the only thing in the world. A tiny outcrop, unnoticed on a sunny day, looms out of the mist as a massive pinnacle. A dinosaur, blocking the way ahead, is transformed, a moment later, into a nervous sheep. Thus acquaintance with the mountains grows into a close relationship, which may develop, as close relationships are wont to do,

---

[1] John and Anne Nuttall (1989) *The Mountains of England and Wales; Volume 1: Wales.* Wales: Cicerone Press

into a vow 'for better or for worse'. Perhaps only one who has developed a love for the mountains could set out on a trip such as this, where, over a five-week period, some of the worse times are inevitable.

Good Friday

The climb onto Cribyn was just as long, steep and eroded as it looked on the way down to the col. At the top, I met a young couple putting on extra sweaters. "It's breezy up here," I greeted them. "Yes, it's a dreadful day," replied the man. I was so astounded by this remark that I made no response. I thought it was a marvellous day. True, the mist had come down again, but not for long. A few moments later, it was torn apart once more to reveal spectacular glimpses of a landscape far more exciting than would appear in unbroken sunshine. I certainly should have said, "A lot better than yesterday."

The ascent to Fan y Big was more or less a twin of the one up Cribyn: just as steep, but with more mud and grass than stones. The top is a spectacular wedge of rock, like the prow of a ship set on a northerly course. It protrudes from the line of the escarpment and gives wonderful views back along the ridge westwards to the highest summits, round which the mist was swirling and lifting even as I stood there trying to catch this dynamic scene in the camera.

I could see also the less dramatic but equally beautiful sweep of the ridge eastwards, which I was to follow next. Amazingly flat-topped, it runs in a great arc for about two miles before the escarpment finally disappears in the grassy slopes of Waun Rydd. No sooner had I embarked on this section than thick mist came down again. The long line of the hill shrank to the span of a few paces, and the steep edge on my left was sensed rather than seen as the ground curved sharply downwards into a uniform grey emptiness. There were fewer people about now, as the highest and most spectacular hills were left behind. I felt privileged to be doing the whole ridge in this way, without the need to return to a vehicle.

A pile of stones covered with blue tarpaulin was obviously intended as an emergency shelter. Inevitably, the area around it was polluted with piles of rotting litter. The next hill lies at the far end of the escarpment, an ill-defined top called Bwlch y Ddwyallt – a misnomer given that 'bwlch' usually refers to a col or a low point on a ridge.

Waun Rydd feels a very different hill. It has two cairns, and the path does not bother to go to the more northerly, which is supposed to be higher. The top is just a plateau of grass and bog, and, although the mist cleared, I felt that the summit could have been almost anywhere. After reaching the southern cairn, I still had to walk quite a long way across this flat terrain on a compass bearing to find the narrow ridge which leads down to the final summit of the Brecon Beacons traverse, Allt Lwyd. This ridge could have been quite tricky to find if the mist had not cleared. Instead, it was tricky because of a strong wind which had blown up unexpectedly. It was now quite clear, but the views of the main ridge were lost on this southern outlier. Most striking now was the view eastwards across Talybont Reservoir with Tor y Foel behind it and the Black Mountains looking a long way off beyond.

I dropped down to the Nant Cynafon and, with some difficulty, found a campsite on its banks. I felt well satisfied with what had started out as a very unpromising day.

10th April

I slept very badly again, but for no apparent reason. In the past, I had usually slept well in a tent and was puzzled by the restless nights I endured in the early part of this walk. There was rather too much darkness perhaps at this time of year, although the radio made it more bearable. As the days grew longer and the nights shorter towards the end of the walk, I spent less time in the tent, slept better and had little time to listen to music.

Certainly, the insomnia was not due to nervousness, for I feel perfectly at home, and happy to be alone, on the empty hillside. Many people seem to find it incomprehensible that one should enjoy walking alone, and the thought of sleeping alone in a tent would simply terrify them. I have walked alone in the hills since I was a teenager, and solitary walking has always been a special delight. Without the distraction of a companion or companions, one feels a much closer rapport with the hills. Fortunately, my husband shares my love of solitude, and we both feel the need to walk alone from time to time. To sleep alone in the mountains is a particular pleasure. One feels a very special affection for a hill after a night in its company. Thus, if anybody asks me which my favourite Munro is, although such a question is really unanswerable, I may well say Carn an Righ. Those who have climbed this hill on an ordinary day, whether in rain or mist or sunshine, might find this an inexplicable choice, but they did not share my secret site where the sun rose over the Cairngorms and mist lay through the Lairig Ghru like the icefall of a mighty glacier. Everyone has their own spectres, I suppose. High on the mountain, I will camp in utter contentment, but I would be frightened to sleep on my own in a bothy.

16th April

It was cloudy but clear, which was helpful in finding a relatively dry route to the two enormous, tidy cairns on Drygarn Fawr. I wondered why this hill should be the one with the smartest summit cairns in the country. Perhaps they were built to celebrate this dry heathery ridge, a little oasis in the midst of a vast area of bog.

What a wonderful, wild and empty area this is. Rowland was surprised when I wrote once that I sometimes feel a touch of fear in empty places, a tingling at the back of the neck I called it. There are places in Scotland where the emptiness clutches you by the throat and becomes in itself almost a threatening presence. Sometimes, you can suddenly stop and the silence is so intense that it assaults the ears as surely as an explosion. I was not feeling that way this morning, for larks and lambs dispersed the silence and ensured a friendly solitude.

I thought of that marvellous verse by Gerard Manley Hopkins, which should be framed on the desk of every National Park and National Trust ranger and engraved on the hearts of all those who are campaigning for long-distance paths and waymarks over the mountains:

What would the world be, once bereft
Of wet and of wildness? Let them be left,
O let them be left, wildness and wet;
Long live the weeds and the wilderness yet.

20ᵗʰ April

I set off in waterproofs again. All went smoothly, although not particularly pleasantly, over the grassy outliers Craig-y-llyn and Tyrrau Mawr in thick mist and cold, driving rain. At least it was beating onto my right shoulder and not driving into my face. I tried to make a beeline for Cyfrwy, which, of course, I could not see, and I probably left the main track too soon, which resulted in unpleasant scrambling over piles of wet and slippery boulders before I joined a cairned route, still very rough, which led to the cairn and wind shelter on this summit.

Now, I had to go out and back to Craig Cwm Amarch, which is on the popular route up from Tal-y-llyn, an ascent which I have done several times. I recollected my first ever climb of Cader Idris with my parents. In those days, it was always spelt in this anglicised way, and we English presumed the Welsh language to be in a state of terminal decline. My father, who preferred lazy beach holidays, which he had enjoyed when we were content to paddle and build sandcastles, suddenly rebelled against being dragged up hills by his offspring and announced, "This will be my last mountain". Later, I came here with Rowland and, for the first time in my life, climbed through the clouds into brilliant sunshine. There was no breath of wind, and just the highest tops could be seen northwards above the sea of cloud. Since then, I have experienced this magic many times, but the first time is always something special. I can still feel the excitement of that day as I gazed spellbound at this unfamiliar aspect of the mountains. We just sat in the sun and stared and stared, locking the scene into our minds as a precious memory, unwilling to descend again into the grey world below.

Today was to become another day to remember, for, as I returned from Craig Cwm Amarch, rifts started to appear in the clouds. There were glimpses of sunny meadows to the west and of the corrie lake, Llyn Cau, seen far below through the swirling mist. Thick mist prevailed at the summit, so I went into the roofed but rather dismal shelter for a belated lunch at about 3 pm. Rain trickled down the walls onto the uninviting benches, and only relief from the bitter wind kept me inside. Still, I do not wholeheartedly approve of a hut in such a situation, and, if it were too comfortable, it would probably attract groups to sleep up there with the attendant problems of litter and vandalism.

When I emerged, I could see Cyfrwy across a swirl of mist. I just had time to get the camera out and photograph it before it vanished again. However, better weather was surely coming, and, by the time I had walked down the east ridge to Mynydd Moel, the sun was shining, although there was still a bitterly cold wind. Looking back, I saw that the highest top was still veiled in mist, but all the others could now be seen, as well as the steep northern escarpment of this magnificent mountain.

28th April

"When the sun shines on the mountain . . . no-one can take my freedom away." The words of a song heard long ago on the radio ran through my head as strolled down the road next morning. Although I have searched through the shelves of country music many times, I have never managed to trace this piece, whose lyrics are so close to my heart. They are often in the heart only – a form of wishful thinking, for freedom is a very elusive thing. Either by choice or by necessity, we all bind ourselves in chains. This walk was indeed a chain of my own making, a chain of 181 links, yet I had seldom felt more carefree, released from the little duties and responsibilities which pressure normal existence. I was granted just an inkling, perhaps, of the paradox of the religious ascetic who finds freedom in bondage and total self-denial.

4th May

Before breakfast, I wandered out to the shores of Llyn Cwellyn, its perfectly smooth surface reflecting the steep slopes of Mynydd Mawr. Only a pair of mallard, paddling slowly in circles, rippled the mirror and set the mountain trembling as I reached for the camera.

I left the hostel at 9 am, having told the warden roughly what I intended to do and warned him not to alert the mountain rescue if I was not back before 9 pm. He laughed and said that I could walk later, with the splendid forecast and the moon nearly at the full.

As I walked up the Snowdon Ranger track, my mind went back nearly 44 years to my first ascent, which was, in fact, my first ascent of *any* mountain – unless you count Selworthy Beacon and Dunkery Beacon on Exmoor as mountains. This climb was done with my parents and my brother, all of them now dead, a fact which filtered a sombre note into my reflections.

When I reached the col above Cwm Brwynog, I could see and hear the train puffing up the track from Llanberis and thought that I could not resent the railway, although it would certainly not be possible to get planning permission for it today. I thought that perhaps when I am too old to walk I might come up here on the train, looking through a mist of tears at this beautiful mountain and recollecting the many times when I walked and scrambled on its magnificent ridges. Perhaps there will be no tears but another moment of joy to be snatched from this lovely hill. Today, the melancholy just brushed the edge of my thoughts, an indulgence to spice my underlying mood of deepest happiness.

The best moment on the Snowdon Ranger route is arrival at the col between Crib y Ddysgl and the highest top, Yr Wyddfa, which reveals a prospect that took my breath away just as surely as it did when I saw it for the first time at the age of thirteen. The ridges of the horseshoe, Crib Goch and Y Lliwedd, enfold the corrie lakes Glaslyn and Llyn Llydaw, with Snowdon summit towering above – surely a scene of mountain beauty to equal any in the world.

A couple met here had come halfway on the train, yet walking from that point they had reached the top long before it. Another young man was already on the summit with a large camera, delighting in the superbly clear conditions. I asked him to photograph me with my little camera, as I felt that this, quite literally high, spot of my walk deserved recording. When he asked me where I had come from, I replied, "Snowdon Ranger", being too modest to answer, "Neath"!

4

The journey from Singapore to Japan

by Gill Frances

My father was one of many men taken prisoner of war in Singapore in February 1942. When he returned to this country in 1945, he brought with him souvenirs and photographs and endless stories about his experiences. Some of these stories entertained my older sisters and me when I was young. As a child of the peace, I inherited the images he had projected of a war which had taken British soldiers raised in the pit towns of Lancashire to places which belonged in picture books. Places where the colours were more vivid than those of home and the temperatures more extreme. I remember him telling me about a mountain called Table Mountain, which looked out over sun-baked soil to an immense, storm-flecked ocean, and showing me pictures he had drawn of the intricate architecture of Indian cities. He told me that, in Japan, the pineapples grew like weeds. Or was that in Singapore? I forget. But I haven't forgotten how astonished I was that Daddy had walked where such exotic plants were common.

He showed me a bracelet he had made out of a kind of soapstone. It must have taken days and days to make, but, as a young child, I was oblivious of the hours of boredom solaced by creativity and only thought how delicate the colours were, and how satisfying was the faint clinking sound they made when you passed them from hand to hand. There was a strange pipe, too, with a long stem and a tiny bowl. I was allowed to handle the pipe and even to sniff the fibres of tobacco Daddy had carefully preserved in a fragile envelope. The smell was almost no smell at all because so much of the fragrance had already vanished into time.

His stories became more vigorous and more challenging as I grew older. Conditions in the POW camps were implied in his descriptions of men being hospitalised with beri-beri, or of young men dying because they didn't know what else to do. When I asked him what he meant by 'not knowing what else to do', he said that the older men were married and had children and desperately wanted to survive in order to ensure their families were safe, whereas the teenagers and men in their early twenties seemed more vulnerable to depression and feelings of hopelessness.

Some of his stories were odd or funny. There was a cook, he said, who stirred a cauldron over an open fire all day and regularly exhorted the men to bring him whatever they scavenged so that he could use their finds to enhance the taste of the stew. It turned out that the cook had been a chef at the Ritz in civilian life. Discussions were heated about which of the ingredients brought to him were responsible for the tantalising flavours of the meagre suppers. Another young man, who suffered from a condition which had rendered him completely hairless, was amazed to find that a fuzzy growth began to appear on his skull after his wig disintegrated in the heat and grit of camp life.

There came a time in my growing up when the things Dad described began to form a coherent narrative in my mind. He was a good story teller who gradually honed his stories to the perfection of performance art, and he dipped into his repertoire to entertain relatives and friends on many occasions. The repetition allowed me to piece together a timeline of sorts. I learned that his journey out to Singapore had been made in great leaps across oceans, first across the Atlantic and back to South Africa, then north to Mombasa and across the Indian

Ocean to Bombay and finally into the Pacific. I understood that he had been immured in three different camps: Changi first, which was within walking distance of Singapore, then Kamiiso on the Japanese island of Hokkaido and, lastly, Nisi-Asabetu, also on Hokkaido. What remained hazy for me until very recently, when I came into possession of his notebooks, was how long he had spent at each camp and how he had been transported from Changi to Kamiiso. Not even when I became a teenager did it occur to me to ask him why he was reticent on this matter. But then, teenagers have more urgent things on their mind.

What is now obvious is that he deliberately obfuscated when it came to describing all the journeys he had made while in Japanese hands. So successfully did he deflect attention from these episodes that, for many years, I had the oddest mental picture of Far Eastern geography. I knew that British prisoners had been marched to Changi from Singapore and imagined that they must have marched from Changi to Hokkaido in similar fashion. It followed that Singapore and Japan were joined together by a land bridge, for how else could the prisoners have walked from one to the other? This childish image of a non-existent Asian continent somehow survived my introduction to atlases and puzzled me at intervals when I could bring myself to think of it. My puzzlement was never articulated, however. Why? Because, although my father was a sociable and talkative person, his silence on this subject was absolute. It repelled curiosity. If you could have thrown a stone into the pool of this silence, you would not have seen a ripple, and, unless he told my mother privately about the crossing to Japan, he mentioned it to no-one. The journey from Singapore to Japan was a lacuna in space and time.

As we girls grew up, my pre-war-vintage sisters dashed ahead of me into the era of boyfriends and make-up and gossip and even the occasional exam. I was in awe of their sudden maturity and grieved for the bike rides and cinema trips they no longer wanted to share. Meanwhile, Dad's war stories passed into ancient history as the house filled with other, and more hormonal, conflicts than those of World War Two. The sketchbooks, notebooks and souvenirs from 1945 were increasingly left undisturbed in a box in the bureau. My father became enthused about working for the union to which he belonged – a surprise to those of us who knew his passionately-held Tory convictions – and teenage rebellions played themselves out in our domestic theatre of war.

Of course, from time to time, we still talked of his experiences as a POW. When I was allowed to read some of the material he kept, I found out that, while in various camps, he had attended lectures on literature, history and science and was deeply grateful to those officers who had chosen to share their knowledge with the men who had had no option but to leave school at the age of 14. But there were lower-brow entertainments, too. Rehearsals for concerts, plays and pantomimes kept everyone busy and gave a structure to the days. My father was discovered to have draftsman's skills and was, on several occasions, occupied in making posters and programmes. I still have the poster for the February 1945 production of *Cinderella* at Nisi-Asibetu. It is an old cement bag, creased and dusty, with Japanese characters on one side and the advertisement for the show with its cast list on the other. My father's name is on the list. It seems he played the Fairy Godmother.

Later still, when we 'girls' were becoming young women, he found it possible to tell us that life as a POW was not all comradeship and optimism. We had realised as much, of course. If nothing else, the films and books of the late Fifties and early Sixties were sufficient to inform us of the atrocities committed in the Far East. But my father, like many men, displayed a kind of gallantry in wanting to protect girls and women from ugly truths for as long as he could. So even as he alluded to the daily humiliations of camp life, the continuous fear of casual physical punishment, the inability of half-starved men to complete factory work and the sad deaths of boys, he softened these accounts by making the allusions fleeting and by jumping quickly to the joy and relief all prisoners felt when the end of the war was announced and food parcels dropped from the sky.

You might expect that this was also the time when he would break his silence about the journey, which, apparently, never happened. But he did not. And neither did we throw a stone into the pool.

***

Two years ago, I inherited custodianship of the wartime materials and, sometime in the course of organising them and transcribing the notes, found two pages in a small notebook listing information in three columns. The first column reads, on alternate lines, 'Left' and 'Arr'. The second column consists of place names. The third column gives dates. It became clear from this information that my father had been in Changi camp for 13 months before being moved on. It seems he left Kepal Harbour, Singapore, on the 16th of May 1943 and arrived in Saigon (Ho Chi Minh City) seven days later. Almost a week after that, he left Saigon and arrived at Formosa (Taiwan) three days later. The next few entries are confusing. It took only two days to reach Japan from Formosa, and the landing place is listed as 'Takow' (Takao) near Tokyo on Honshu, from which (if this is correct) he must have gone south to Moji and then to nearby Shimonoseki on Kyushu Island before making the final trip north to Hakodate on the island of Hokkaido. The whole journey, if the dates are to be trusted, lasted 21 days, at least 10 or 11 of which were spent on board ship. There is no mention of prisoners spending time anywhere other than on the vessel.

At this point, it occurred to me to do what one of my grandchildren would have done straight away: I switched on the computer and googled 'British prisoners of war in Japan'. And, within a few minutes of starting to read, I encountered, for the first time, the phrase 'hell ships'.

It took very little time to establish that the ship which left Singapore in May '43 was the Wales (or Weills) Maru, a cargo vessel designed to be crewed by around 13 or 14 men. Nine hundred and fifty prisoners of war were crammed onto the ship, 600 of them British, 300 Australian and the rest of unspecified, but quite possibly Dutch, nationality. Various internet sources make it clear that conditions on board the hell ships were indescribably bad. There were nowhere near the number of latrines required for so many men, water was scarce and food scarcer. There was little room to lie down. If Allied vessels were sighted, the hatches were battened down. Prisoners died of dysentery, exhaustion, starvation and asphyxiation. One survivor told of seeing men in a dreamlike state, the lack of oxygen, perhaps mercifully, robbing them of full consciousness.

I found it impossible to visualise my father in the midst of this hell. I clung to the images of his war experiences formed in my mind over decades: I could imagine him slogging through the Changi days, getting over the anger and bitterness that followed the surrender and making the best of it. I could imagine him attempting, and failing, to keep up with the work demanded of him in the cement factory on Hokkaido. I could see him in my mind's eye tired, ill, grey faced, with the marks of beatings on him. I could appreciate that he had utilised every weapon in the armoury of a prisoner to fight the demons of depression and despair so that he could find his way home. But I could not picture him inhabiting this desperate nightmare in which, for days and weeks on end, each breath he drew must have contained within it the possibility of its being his last. I could not, and still cannot, understand the qualities of mind necessary to survive such treatment.

However, I think I do understand that, in order for a person to survive such an experience in the longer term, their mind might refuse to process it in the normal way. I think my father sealed it off in a mental cul-de-sac and refused to put it into words. I think he knew that, if he turned the experience into a story, he would risk being destroyed by the horror of it at every telling. And so he remained silent.

***

My father believed in getting on with life. Much though he enjoyed his story-telling, he never conveyed the slightest hint, when talking about the war, that he had been emotionally damaged by it. He remained angry at the ineptitude of the British High Command in causing hundreds of men to be disembarked in Singapore on the 10th February 1942 only to surrender them into enemy hands five days later, but any resentment he felt against the Japanese seemed to find expression only in a mild determination not to buy a Toyota.

And there it is. Like many children, I did not ask the right questions when my father was alive and could answer them. In fact, as a teenager, I remember feeling guiltily bored sometimes when he reminisced and wished I could read my book or listen to Radio Luxembourg instead of politely paying attention. Even as an adult, I was hesitant about awakening monsters from the depths of the eastern seas. For his part, Dad was wary of voluntarily imagining himself back on the Wales Maru. The result is that, between us, we colluded to shield ourselves from an unutterable truth and created a lacuna – not between Singapore and Japan but between the generations.

Perhaps such collusion is not unusual. Perhaps the most profound understanding between parent and child lies in what is unspoken rather than in what is said. What *is* certain is that what he felt about his experience on the Wales Maru is now forever out of reach. And, sometimes, I feel sad about my part in that loss, which explains why, especially when I drive my Honda round town, I find myself saying a mental 'sorry' from time to time to the friendly and forgiving ghost in my head.

5

Mercy mission to Romania

by Jean Gallagher

We stood on the edge of the abyss, and our hearts sank: no way would we get our vehicles over that narrow gorge which, though only about six feet wide, seemed bottomless. Anything which fell down there, be it man or beast, would never return to see the light of day. Were all our months of preparation and hard work to be in vain? As we stood and pondered on what best to do, a thin drizzly rain began to fall.

The drive across Europe in early May had been superb. Blue skies, warm sunshine, wonderful scenery, genuine comradeship, as seven groups of four people, mostly strangers, melded together into close units to work for three weeks in an alien environment. It had all started six months earlier, when the guns began to fire on that cold December day, and the people of Romania revolted against the oppressive regime which had made their lives a living hell and which we, cosseted in the affluent West, couldn't begin to comprehend.

When the first pictures of the horrific conditions in the orphanages reached our television screens, I felt in my heart of hearts that I would somehow become involved. I was on the edge of a new life. My children and husband were gone, and I faced an uncertain future. I was on the edge of – what? Events unfolded quickly. I heard of a meeting to be held in Carlisle for anyone interested in helping with providing aid to Rumania. Off I went, nervously standing at the edge of a group of about a hundred people, with not a familiar face in sight.

We were invited to sit down at long tables and given bowls of steaming hot soup (delicious it was) and crusty home-made bread. Everyone was very friendly. I was sitting next to a nurse who had been caring for the terminally ill in Yorkshire. There were a lot of medical people from all over the North of England and from Scotland. The organisers needed 28 skilled people to work in teams of four: doctors, nurses, engineers, carpenters, plumbers, decorators and others. On the form we had been given, we had to provide our details, such as our background and what skills we thought we could offer, as well as the reason why we wanted to go. I handed my form in thinking: well, that's it! They won't want me. But a few days later, to my great surprise, I had a phone call asking if I would be prepared to help organise the aid at this end and the distribution at the other, to which I readily agreed.

Leading the convoy out of Carlisle, May 1991

Distributing aid

Beyond the Misty Fells

The project was truly exhilarating. One's faith in humanity was restored as the gifts poured in from all sides: large firms, small firms, individuals and groups from Brownie packs to WIs. Cumbria County Council lent two wagons, a garage loaned a new Mercedes transit van; I was one of the lucky ones assigned to drive it. We soon had seven vehicles, all the petrol we needed, free crossings of the Channel from Sally Line and free accommodation at various points across Europe provided by the Red Cross. As we crossed the border from Austria into Hungary, the tarmac ended and we knew that we had come to the edge of the world we knew as the flat lands of Hungary drew us into a world that seemed hardly to have changed since mediaeval times.

But now, we stood helplessly peering into the gorge, and it looked as though we could go no further. Suddenly, we heard some shouts, and out of the mist and rain appeared about a dozen young men. They did not speak any language we recognised but appeared to be assessing the situation and indicated that they would return before disappearing into the gloom. True to their word, they reappeared dragging huge tree trunks, which they proceeded to throw across the gorge. Seven brave souls inched the huge pantechnicons across, while the rest of us went on foot. (I had never been more terrified in my life.)

We soon reached our destination – a village in the foothills of the mountains of Transylvania, where we stayed for three days. We were beginning to feel very hungry: our supplies of fresh fruit were long gone, and the meals provided by our hosts were so meagre that many of us were beginning to suffer from upset tummies. So it was with great pleasure that we accepted an invitation to an evening meal at the village a few miles away. We set off with half a dozen of young men who were to be our guides towards a steep gully with a little stream meandering slowly down. I enjoyed the walk and, as it got steeper and more rocky, was thankful that I was fit enough to keep up with the leaders – others found it more difficult.

Our young guides bounded backwards and forwards, encouraging the laggards and laughing and joking among themselves. They all carried fearsome-looking knives and kept uprooting young saplings and whittling off the bark – real rascals I thought, glad that there were twenty six of us if trouble should ensue.

Eventually, after a strenuous two hours, we reached a flat grassy plateau. A few scraggy sheep grazed at the far end, and a tiny wooden shack stood at the edge. The rain was falling steadily now. As we stood around, the young men dug a pit about a foot deep and covered it with the saplings they had cut as we were negotiating the gorge. They slaughtered a sheep by cutting its throat and collected its blood in an enamel dish. A fire was lit in the pit – no mean feat, as it was still pouring with rain and there did not appear to be any matches. The sheep was quickly skinned and roasted, fresh trout appeared from inside someone's coat, wine was poured over it on the spit, and, under a tree in the far corner of the field, we had one of the best suppers I had ever had in my life, washed down with the local plum brandy. As night fell, much inebriated we took the downward path in the direction of our beds in the next village.

This trek was a nightmare. People slipped and stumbled down the gorge, where the stream had become a rushing torrent. Margaret (a nurse from Carlisle Hospital) fell and broke a leg. She thus had to be carried for the rest of the journey and helped to bed. With her and me sharing a room, there was no sleep for either of us. The doctors had decided that she needed an urgent operation, so plans were changed: we needed to go back to England straight away.

In the morning, we began the journey back home. First, we had to traverse the terrifying gorge using the same tree trunks, which were still in place. We travelled for three days, stopping only for comfort breaks. Returning home was wonderful: running water, clean beds and decent healthcare. The organiser asked me to go again, but I said no. The heart problems that would result in surgery five years later were slowing me down, and I feared that I might be too much of a liability. With more and more people becoming involved, the convoys continued, and I hoped that, with the expansion of the European Union, the lot of these people would slowly improve.

6

An alien's English odyssey

by Anna Nolan

"I'll pay for the cruise if it's the last thing I do!" declared my mother, an ardent Anglophile, rather effusively. The cold war was on, the iron curtain was down, communism was in full swing and the free world was out of reach to us Poles. But she was head over heels in passion with the English language and worshipped a small island hanging off the western edge of Europe and, somewhat confusingly, concealing its greatness behind the white cliffs of Dover. Seeing as we were firmly in the grip of communism's tentacles and couldn't wriggle free to travel to the West, my mother hatched a cunning plan: she would send me on a cruise taking in the English Channel so that I would at least be able to catch a glimpse of the famous cliffs, which, to her, symbolised Britain. Granted, I wouldn't be allowed to disembark, but my simply feasting on the sight of the island so revered by her would, she decided, be enough.

Although I never did go on that cruise, I nevertheless studiously devoured English and its grammar and, like my mother, fell hopelessly in love with the language, which would become the great passion of my life that would eventually lead me to Britain – and to this book.

Getting to this juncture had been a long, circuitous and bumpy ride, though. The English textbooks of yore, which were a veritable font of knowledge about those faraway islands, depicted a baffling but oh-so-tantalising world inhabited by moustachioed gentlemen invariably called Mr Black or Mr Brown, who always wore bowler-hats and pinstripe suits and carried umbrellas. I remember wondering whether these umbrellas offered adequate protection against the cats and dogs which were apparently always raining down on them. The sugar-coated ladies in frilly pinnies were continually rustling up heavenly delights, and the beaming and well-scrubbed kiddies at their knee were, without exception, referred to as 'merry and gay'. I couldn't quite understand why, when I finally made it to Britain in the early Eighties, I'd get filthy looks off blithe young gentlemen, otherwise perfectly agreeable, whenever I complimented them on their exuberance with the entirely fitting – or so I thought – "My, you are so gay!", but that's by the by.

But even such wholesome-looking people as those depicted in my English textbooks would evidently get peeved from time to time, and I formed the impression that they would then let off steam by kicking either the bucket or themselves. Oh, and they'd also kick the habit. I wasn't thus in the least surprised that their dialogue was peppered with the interjections "My foot!", as foot injury must have been an inevitable consequence of such outbursts. If you discounted those who didn't have a leg to stand on, that is. And, judging by how often they would spill the beans, they seemed to me rather clumsy. On the other hand, they'd get on their high horse without falling off, so I failed to reach a definite conclusion one way or the other.

I also wondered why they were so fond of expressing themselves cryptically: you see, while they would say "Come through", they would never explain through *what* exactly. Or whenever they announced they had fallen over, they kept you guessing as to over *what* exactly they had fallen. And why did they never give you a straight answer to "How do you do?" Such a perfectly straightforward question, you would think, yet they never actually explained *how* they did. But that's not all – far from it.

Beyond the Misty Fells

Apparently, everybody in Britain always talked about the weather. And they had some very interesting national dishes incorporating cool cucumbers, keen mustard and red herring. Why, when they had such delicacies, they'd also eat their hats seemed entirely unfathomable. Then again, they appeared to harbour a strange dislike of the old hat, so maybe that's why. And, of course, they drove on the wrong side of the road, which – to them – was right, although it was actually left. Another unsolved mystery was why they would stuff their fish into kettles. Confronted by such eccentricities, I felt I had no option but to try to read between the lines. Imagine my relief when I realised that, despite their frequent references to pet hate, they didn't really hate pets all that much – certainly not the top dog or mother hen. On the other hand, they did chase wild geese and seem strangely reluctant to be sold a pup. And I must admit that their practice of skinning the cat appeared to me thoroughly repugnant, but they made up for that somehow by organising parties for stags and hens.

Their eccentricity notwithstanding, most of them seemed kindly, polite (it was only their health that was rude) and beguiling, so I grew up with the notion of a genial, though decidedly quirky, people who spoke a difficult but fascinating language which was hard to write and even harder to pronounce and where every rule had umpteen exceptions. Little wonder that, to me, Britain was mysterious, intriguing and alluring; it was also tantalisingly out of reach.

But, finally, when your border guards happened to be on a fag break, I managed to sneak into this great country (that your border controls were lax even then is incontrovertible). Imagine my delight when, at long last, I was able to delve deeply into the British psyche. Take the writing on the wall, for example. Since the lovely natives always uttered this phrase in grave tones, I was able to deduce that, like me, they didn't approve of graffiti. And when you heard that they were always getting a third degree, you couldn't help but be awed by their putting such great store by higher education. Needless to say, I was deeply touched by their enthusiastic "You can say that again", with which they were always letting me know that they simply couldn't get enough of my exotic accent. Charming people! And very, very helpful when it came to giving directions: they were always telling you where to get off. And what amazing generosity: they would even lend you their ear!

Anyway, lady luck had undoubtedly smiled on me, allowing me to put down roots in this wonderful country and to indulge my all-consuming passion for English with utter abandon. After a spell as a teacher of English and broadcaster at the Polish Section of the BBC, I enjoyed many adrenaline-charged years running public examinations, developing different types of qualifications for both English and Scottish authorities, carrying out linguistic research, copy-editing and penning articles and books on English grammar, punctuation and usage. I also produce a blog, Flaming English, in which I write on the subject, alternating between jocularity and sobriety. My website/ blog, which has scored hits all over the world, can be found at: http://flaming-english.com/.

And it is the skits from this blog that form my section of this book. The sketches, representative of my frolicsome style, offer a glimpse into my weird inner world, where humour and grammar blend into a whimsical mix. The first is coming right up.

The elusive comma

Over 30 years ago, when I was a greenhorn in Britain and still in the state of more or less permanent bewilderment, I was mightily chuffed as the recipient of a carefully crafted message which ended on this pleasing note:

Brilliant Anna!

Having never doubted my own splendidness, I was nevertheless gratified to have this quality unequivocally confirmed by an independent third party – and a *real* Briton at that! It was only later, when I started getting to grips with the natives' idiosyncratic ways of wielding their language, that it dawned on me that what the sender, with whom I had previously been engaged in a professional colloquy, had been trying to articulate was this:

Brilliant, Anna!

Still not bad, of course, but the marvelousness was, apparently, being attributed merely to what I had said in the course of our confabulation rather than to the whole package. Oh well, so that's another illusion shattered then.

That my esteemed interlocutor was not entirely *au fait* with the comma could not be doubted – and he didn't appear to be the only one, even though this helpful punctuation mark has many important uses: I have identified 17 key ones. The chief among them is to prevent misinterpretation when we address people and other living creatures. Consider the meaning conveyed by the following pairs of sentences.

Kill, Rex!
Kill Rex!

They are attacking, Pete.
They are attacking Pete.

These are good, folk.
These are good folk.

Take that, Boris.
Take that Boris.

Follow them, guys.
Follow them guys.

Let's eat, granny.
Let's eat granny.

In other words, a comma is ALWAYS used when we address somebody or something in writing. Correction, not always – in fact, it often isn't. But it certainly should be. Otherwise, the fate of the unfortunate granny wouldn't even bear contemplating.

7

The bike ride

by Christine Mitchell

Being very flat, Southport is a place for bikes, so we all rode bikes from infancy onwards. Mum hated bikes; ever since she had fallen off one as a child, she thought they were dangerous. One Sunday, Dad proposed taking us on a bike ride. Mum reluctantly said all right, as long as we were back for Sunday lunch, at 2.30 pm.

It was Dad's favourite bike ride, not mine, may I add. It was a sunny Sunday in the school holidays. We had spent the previous day cleaning our bikes under Dad's strict supervision. In the morning, we set off along quiet suburban back roads until we met the main road into Southport, which was choc-a-bloc with visitors heading to and from the seaside resort.

We wended our way down the main road, like sheep following their leader. Dad was first, then the eldest brother Bob on his full-size bike, sister Gill third on her medium-size bike and me last on my small bike. I was wobbling nervously, as my wheels were very close to the continuous traffic roaring on the busy road. We were heading for the Leeds Liverpool canal, about five miles out of town.

For us children, the canal was our main objective. Dad, as we well knew from past experience, had a different one. There was a famous watering hole, called the Houseboat, adjacent to the canal. We were not surprised when we parked our bikes against the hostelry. Dad went inside. At this time, there were no special rooms for children in public houses, or seats outside to sit on. So we sat on the steps and ground outside, watching the boats, but were not forgotten. Our sustenance of pop and crisps soon arrived. We were not looking forward to our return journey in the traffic.

After over an hour, Father appeared, looking like an overripe Braeburn apple, certainly considerably rosier than an hour ago. "I have found a new route home," he announced. "The landlord told me we can ride on the toll path for a couple of miles, then veer off across the fields to the outskirts of the town."

With considerable relief, we set off along the toll path. The path was rutted and a bit muddy, but it was much preferable to dodging cars. After a couple of miles, we all cast about for any sign of a track across the fields. "Look, that must be it!" shouted Bob, pointing to a raised embankment a hundred yards away. Unfortunately, the one hundred yards consisted of mud, brambles and rosebay willow herb. Undaunted, and relieved to find a way off the canal track, Dad led us through.

We finally reached the embankment, caked in various degrees of mud. Father was coated up to his knees, me up to my waist. Our once-clean bikes were unrecognisable, except as wrecks washed up by the tide. The embankment too was muddy, so each back tyre threw mud onto the rider behind. Being the last, and low down on a small bike, I received the most despoliation. I dared not open my mouth, my red hair was caked in grey-brown mud, my eyes were just visible. Riding the embankment, we must have looked like trolls out of their element on a lunar landscape of ploughed fields. Eventually, we found some minor roads home. None of us wished to be seen by anyone in our present, disreputable, condition.

Arriving late for Mum's Sunday lunch, we were starving. Mum took one look at us and announced, "You're not coming into my clean house trampling in all that mud; you'll have to be hosed down outside." We stripped to our underwear whilst Dad hosed us and our bikes down with cold water. He later swilled himself down in the washhouse.

After changing into clean clothes, we tucked into a rather dried-up Sunday lunch of roast beef, Yorkshire puddings and roast potatoes, followed by apple crumble and custard. Mum was very disappointed about the lunch, but, with our rumbling tummies, it tasted like the greatest banquet ever. Dad was, of course, blamed for the state we were in. Mum had the last word, saying, "I told you nothing good would come of all this bike-riding: it's not safe, it only gives me a load of extra washing to do, and you've spoilt my lunch."

8

Bumping along in Botswana

by John Howell

Camping right by the shores of the swamps of the Okavango Delta in Botswana, we were in the middle of hippo country. During the day, the hippos stood almost submerged in the swamp, doing absolutely nothing, with just nose, eyes and ears peeping above the waterline. At night, however, they would suddenly come to life, bursting into song – not *Mud Mud* … but rather a gentle humming – before clambering out onto the bank to go grazing. You could hear them tramping about and marking their territory. This involved defecating whilst they whizzed their tail rapidly back and forth to create not only a loud whirring noise but a well-spread territorial message. In spite of their bulk, they were nervous out of the water and, at the first sign of danger, would take the shortest route to the swamp, ignoring anything in their path, which was simply run over.

The camping facilities for the four of us comprised one tent pitched on the ground and another which unfolded on top of our Land Rover and which was accessed by a rickety steel ladder. Age being what it is, nightly excursions to ground level were usually essential, and, after keeping a wary ear open for tromping and chomping noises, one descended, took a few steps away from the vehicle in consideration of the other occupant, did what one had to do without any accompanying whirring noise and scuttled back up the ladder. The following morning, it was sobering to find large hippo tracks going back to the swamp right where our nightly excursion had occurred. Other tales of the risks of

40

camping abounded amongst the campers, generally involving a lion or hyenas and, of course, a careless camper who had let their foot stray outside the zipped confines of the tent whilst asleep.

We were in Botswana with our former neighbours from Wiltshire, Pam and Dick, who had recently spent a couple of years teaching there. On their return, they offered to go back to Botswana with us on a self-drive safari, with an itinerary planned by Safari Drive, a company based in Lambourn, Wiltshire. The company pre-booked us into the park campsites and a few lodges as well as providing a superbly equipped Land Rover Defender and maps; now, they would also provide satellite phones and GPS. We, however, were quite comfortable with old-fashioned paper maps. They are quite useful and somehow more confidence-inspiring – so long as the features on the ground approximate to those on the map closely enough.

We jumped at Pam and Dick's offer and promptly signed ourselves up for off-road 4WD driving instruction, which took place on the Greystoke estate. Not only was this great fun, but it taught us to place a lot of faith in our vehicle. When we arrived at Maun airport near the Okavango Delta, we were met by the company guide, who showed us our vehicle equipped with everything, including a kitchen sink (canvas, naturally). There was a good supply of iron rations (in cans) plus dry goods in boxes, and we duly filled up with perishables and a bottle or two from the local stores before setting off for the bush.

After about 100 kilometres heading towards the national park on a decent road, we turned off onto a dirt track and, just after crossing the park boundary, had a puncture. Changing the wheel on a Land Rover sitting on sand is an operation which had not been covered on our training course: the jack simply sank into the ground instead of lifting the jeep. After a lot of scrabbling amongst the assorted camping gear in the vehicle, which was gradually laid out on the road, we realised that we were actually within an area where it was strictly forbidden to get out of the vehicle due to unpredictable local inhabitants (of the four-footed variety). Intensifying the search, we discovered a sort of thick rubber mat, and, with the aid of the mat and some tin plates, got the wheel off the ground and changed.

Changing the wheel

Mobile again, we soon reached the first night's camp: the free Okavango Delta Moremi Camp; nearby was a fenced enclosure where the richer tourists were camping in wooden lodges, fully catered for and with armed guides all around. We set up camp around a rather rickety stone fireplace equipped with a bent grill and a waste bin hanging by a chain from a tree. Carefully avoiding positioning ourselves under a tree which was covered in large nut-like objects called sausage fruits, each about 0.5 metres long, 7 centimetres in diameter and weighing a kilogram or so, we watched some of them fall to earth with a thump more frequently than we would have liked.

Sausage fruits on the ground

We were surrounded by monkeys and small baboons. They watched us setting up camp and preparing our meal, then chose a moment when Patricia was the only one around, the rest of us having headed off in search of firewood. A sudden dart from one monkey towards the jeep prompted Patricia to run over and chase it away, leaving the next one free rein on the supper table, where the chief target was a pot of yoghurt. We learnt quickly and extracted a catapult from the supplied gear. It was discovered that the mere act of pulling one's hand back without actually loading the weapon produced a scattering to the trees. Surprisingly, we slept well.

We started our journey by entering the Okavango Delta Moremi Game Reserve and then following the Chobe River along the Savuti Channel as far as the Zambezi, where we would cross into Zambia to get the best view of the Victoria Falls. Along the way, we would mostly camp, but we also had some R&R nights planned in safari lodges so that we could get a shower and some more adventurous fare than that which we could rustle up from the dried and canned ingredients we had assembled before the trip. Fortunately, these lodges were very comfortable, even the one which was totally under canvas. Each tent was enormous, with a power supply, a wooden floor, a full-height shower and a toilet area.

The lodges laid on sunrise and sunset excursions with knowledgeable guides, who knew where to find many of the more interesting animals. However, Dick had studied the local birds while teaching near the capital, Gaborone, and could reel off most of their names with great aplomb. It was a matter of pride to try to catch up a little and then make sure of identifying at least those hopping around our tents. The range of bird species is enormous, and we were privileged to see a wide selection, from the tiny little bee-eaters and the lilac-breasted rollers to the larger sacred ibises and wattled cranes. There were several varieties of hornbills, with the turkey-sized and fearsome-looking ground hornbill dwarfing the others.

Ground hornbills

Beyond the Misty Fells

A typical day would start early with a drive around the area surrounding our camp. For obvious reasons, we would not leave the vehicle but mounted a camera onto an open window. A decent telephoto lens offered an excellent chance of memorable shots. We would stop at suitable vantage points, usually completely on our own, unless we happened to be near a lodge. Sitting in the Land Rover and watching the animals, sometimes over quite extended periods, allowed some close observation of their habits and peculiarities.

Cape buffalo looking through the window

The first morning after we arrived at the Moremi Game Reserve was opportunistic in that we tagged onto a group of vehicles purposefully emerging from a nearby luxury camp. Suddenly, they came to an abrupt halt. Looking out of my window, I found myself within a metre of the enormous head of a Cape buffalo with its formidable curved horns. Having watched the herd for some time, we had to reverse and retrace our steps. A fairly sedate drive around the area followed, with us spotting grazing impala, zebra and kudu, which we could pass fairly close by. Eventually, we returned to our campsite – only to catch a glimpse of a leopard. As these are difficult animals to see, we counted ourselves quite fortunate. The leopard simply crossed the track in front of us and proceeded along, paying us no attention whatsoever.

From the Moremi Game Reserve, we moved into the Savuti Channel and then the Chobe National Park. Along the way, we encountered numerous herds of elephants and watched them at the watering holes. Intriguingly, the herds, each headed by the matriarch, came to the water one by one. They drank, the youngsters played about in the deeper water, and then they moved off, and the next herd, which had been waiting out of sight in the bush, strolled down to take its turn. Once, we were somewhat alarmed to find ourselves on a narrow track between two different herds. They were going about their business, strolling gently along the pathway, browsing, getting closer and, apparently, growing bigger. We just stayed put, and they kept out of our way, gradually disappearing back into the bush; we could move on.

Giraffes lolloping along

Beyond the Misty Fells

Along the river, there was an island apparently favoured by about a dozen thirsty giraffes. The island was very low lying and must have held water pools. Giraffes are browsers which like to nibble on the topmost leaves and shoots of the thorny acacia trees. To do that, they must have tongues that are remarkably robust. When it comes to drinking, however, giraffes are at a considerable disadvantage. They spread their legs further and further apart until, eventually, they can reach the ground or the surface of the pool and drink. Having satisfied their thirst, they would reassemble in long gangly lines and lollop away, still holding their elegant heads high.

A well-surfaced park road goes very close to the Chobe River, and so we could see numerous birds by the water's edge. They are often standing in the water catching fish. We managed to photograph both a great egret and a wattled crane in the act of swallowing remarkably large fish.

Great egret with fish

There were regular sightings of the African darter or snake bird, so called because it hunts swimming in the water, with only its head and long neck sticking out, looking for all the world like a water snake. Having finished a watery patrol, the darter pulls itself out of the water and spreads its wings to dry in the sun.

African darter drying its wings

In a pond near the river, there were hippos, standing in the mud, only eyes and ears showing above the water. A pair of saddle-backed storks stood by the edge of the pond, their yellow beaks saddled in the middle with a dark band. We drove on until we spotted any behaviour that was different or just simply amazing. We came across an elephant graveyard, massive skulls bleached in the sun and picked clean by the variety of carrion eaters.

At one camp, there was a stone fireplace with a cooking grate cemented in but even more twisted and deformed than our usual ones, possibly from an errant vehicle or a clumsy hippo. Nevertheless, it was quite capable of supporting a kettle and cooking a meal.

Camp fireplace

As with all self-catering camping trips, the business of coping with survival and food is not really difficult, but it is time consuming. Campsites rarely have sufficient firewood, and, if no large animals are about, it is sensible to pick some up during the day. We would tie great bundles onto our roof rack and take it with us to the next camp.

Tying the firewood to the roof rack

There, we would ferret around in the food supply in the back of our Land Rover and devise a menu with a slight variation on corned beef or tuna with reconstituted mashed potato. Then, after supper, there was time to watch the bird-life around the camp itself. Usually, there will be one or more little bee-eaters with yellow breasts and bright brown head, possibly a black-collared red-headed barbet and even, occasionally, a lilac-breasted roller. They would come quite close and pose prettily for their photographs.

A buffalo happened to reside very close to where we decided to pitch our next camp. He was a solitary male, young, apparently rather sad and quite docile, though one needs to be very wary of the species. We put up our tents close to the water and watched him graze. Then, noticing a standpipe nearby fed by a black polythene pipe, we found that it gave forth very hot sun-heated water. Our vehicle was equipped with a shower bucket, which was promptly filled with the hot water, and I treated myself to an *al fresco* shower but could not persuade my fellow campers of its delights. There were supposed to be solar hot-water panels on the toilet block, but we were darkly told that the Namibians cross the river at night to remove the panels as booty.

When we stayed at a safari lodge, there was always the chance of a proper hot shower, luxury bedding and someone else cooking supper. The camps varied; the one under canvas I have already described. Another had a large open balcony on which dinner was served. It looked directly out onto a waterhole where numerous elephants were gathered. There were also some antelope there and, of course, many birds. In the evening, just before sunset, we drove out in a viewing vehicle with high-level seats and a knowledgeable guide. He stopped to show us a small indentation in the sand, which, he claimed, had been made by a lion's paw. It was the closest we came to a lion on the whole trip, at least as far as we were aware.

Gnu between elephants

Beyond the Misty Fells

We stopped to watch a herd of elephants desperately pawing the ground to find water. In amongst them, looking really tiny, was a gnu – on its own, it appears a respectable size, but here it simply emphasized how large elephants are. Diminutive warthogs snuffled around near some banded mongooses (or is it mongeese?), which were tinier still. The elephants not being accompanied by more dangerous beasts, we were allowed to alight from the vehicle. The guide solemnly declared it was time for the African custom of sundowners, which implies almost any alcoholic drink poured ceremoniously into a suitable container – in our case, teacups.

Savouring a sundowner

The surrounding landscape was quite barren except for a few dry waterholes and one or two baobab trees. These trees have enormous trunks topped by a small knot of green foliage.

Beyond the Misty Fells

Baobab tree

The baobabs are a signature sight in that region and as dramatic as the trees where weaver birds build their grey mud nests. With their distinctive hanging dwellings, whole flocks colonise just a few trees.

We reached the end of the Chobe River as it merged into the much bigger Zambezi. Here, four countries meet: Botswana, Namibia, Zambia and Zimbabwe. Crocodiles could occasionally be seen on the river banks now. We were going to cross into Zambia to view the Victoria Falls; crossing the Zambezi would be by ferry. Arriving at the crossing point, we were confronted by a short line of trucks and cars and a group of young men who offered to navigate us through the intricacies of entering Zambia. We were led to believe this would be quite difficult but told not to worry, as they would handle the necessary paperwork; we should thus be thankful that the formalities would be taken care of. We weighed up the pros and cons: the cost seemed reasonable and the advantages significant. We struck a deal with someone who appeared to be fairly senior in the group and who agreed to sort us out. We then boarded the ferry and set sail across some 100 metres of water.

On the other side, we disembarked into a semi-fenced area with several single-storey grey concrete buildings at one side, into which our *despachante* vanished. The '*despachante*' is a respected professional in Brazil, where, on retiring, officials from government and other bureaucratic agencies take up the profession of easing one through the bureaucracy for a fee which is directly related to the height of the pile of red tape they had been busily building up in their former life. Our man in Livingston, for that was the town near the border post, vanished into a queue, then another one; I kept a weather eye on him, tracking his oscillations around the various stations until he reappeared bearing passports and a bill for the visas or permits – whatever it was we were receiving. One mysterious item was the 'climate change charge'. We asked what the money would be used for and were told that it was to be used by the president. The '*despachante*' did not ask for a specific sum – he merely suggested "whatever you would like to give me". He was happy, we were happy, and we proceeded to Livingston.

In Livingston, we needed petrol and pulled into a garage to fill up. The attendant informed us that we had a flat tyre. In fact, it was possible to watch it gently deflate. Well, this was a much more apposite location than that of our previous flat in the deep bush on the first day. We got this one sorted professionally on the spot and sought out our refuge for the night. Our instructions for the night's oasis were rather vague: a statement that x kilometres from the outskirts of the town there would be a dirt road to the left, which we were to follow to reach the safari lodge. We must have missed it because the next sight was the column of spray from Victoria Falls to the right and the Zimbabwe border dead ahead. Unwilling to sample Mugabe hospitality, we retraced our steps, and, by dint of more careful study of the instructions, now of course to be read in reverse, located the dirt road. We were thus able to proceed to the lodge, and what a lodge it was. Each couple had a small open-plan apartment facing the distant sight of the spray from the falls. The whole falls-facing side of the building was open, and we had a full en-suite facility, with a restaurant close by or the option of a meal in our quarters. What luxury! We had hot showers, full beds and clean sheets and bedding, no ladder to climb down in the middle of the night and only a small selection of the minor menagerie of the country. English was spoken fluently, and we relaxed.

Victoria Falls

The proprietor explained that they were trying to be as self-sufficient as possible and, besides trying to rely on local produce, they used some of the profits to support a local village, which they urged us to visit. On arriving in the village, only a couple of kilometres from our luxury lodge, we saw a queue for water, which consisted of a very orderly line of water pots. No owners were in evidence – unless it was a selection of them sitting under a nearby tree. Clearly, although the mighty Zambezi thundered down within sight, water was here a much prized commodity to be savoured in small potfuls whenever the opportunity arose.

The villagers had trinkets for sale, but, although we bought some, they were not of much intrinsic value and appeared to have been manufactured specifically to a modern design rather than representing the indigenous culture.

In the morning, we visited the Victoria Falls and walked down into the gorge and then across a promontory which sat in the full spray of the water. The river Zambezi pours over a lip of rock some 400 metres long and crashes into the gorge 100 metres below, creating a dense mist of spray. Umbrellas were available for hire, and we enjoyed a couple of hours wandering around. At sunset, we gathered to watch the sun sink over the falls and found ourselves in the middle of a French film crew, some of whom were eager to take still pictures from the same spot we had chosen. The sunlight goes quickly in Africa, and soon we were off to dine in luxury.

For the next adventure, two of us went canoeing on the Zambezi River above the falls. As we drifted down the river, the guide stood up in his canoe to keep a wary eye out for crocodiles and, more importantly, hippos, which are a much greater problem to the canoeist. The crocodiles will eat you only after the hippos have tipped you into the water. Lunch was taken on the right bank of the river, in Zimbabwe, where our guide muttered darkly that the most dangerous animal in those parts was a Mugabe. He himself was a Zimbabwean exile and still had family there.

Beyond the Misty Fells

The final part of the trip after passing the north edge of the Kalahari – home to the San people – involved a visit to the Tsodilo Hills near the town of Shakawe. The Tsodilo Hills, a World Heritage site, used to be home to the San people, who left behind over 4,500 rock paintings. These were described by Laurens van der Post; some have been dated as being over 24,000 years old. Some of the paintings are quite explicit, the male figures being exceptionally well endowed.

Old San rock paintings

The hills are scarred by the grooves worn by cattle being brought down for water by the San over the millennia.

Grooves in solid rock worn by cattle

Now, there is almost no San settlement nearby except for a handful of San people employed by the national park. Overall, the Botswanan government has not treated the San well, and they are now being banned from hunting in the Kalahari, their homeland. When they are caught following their traditional way of life, they are likely to be badly beaten. Great pity, for it seems to outsiders a gentle country, depicted as such in Alexander McCall's books with their traditionally-built lady detective.

It was now time to return to Maun for the flight home. Past the edge of the Kalahari, we passed an area of completely flat desert, noting from the map that there should be a lake in the vicinity. Having made the short detour required to reach the lake, we could see through our binoculars a massive flock of pink flamingos feeding in the water. They seemed to us aloof, unreachable and somehow mystical. Taking our last farewell of the rich wildlife between the desert and the swamp, we wondered how the future of this welcoming country would unfold.

9

A surreal day in Lyme Regis

by Aline Hopkins

They say that stones choose you, not you them. It has something to do, apparently, with the way everything in the universe resonates at a specific frequency, a unique musical affinity.

I was in Lyme Regis, a place with millions, possibly billions, of stones, as far as the eye could see along the beach in each direction. The beach looked promising. Myriad shades of grey dappled the pebbles and made a seamless transition across the promenade and the stone walls of the houses of the town. How would one find me from so many?

A long time ago, the stones here gave up their secrets to a young girl, Mary Anning, presenting her with a massive fossil of some prehistoric creature. This now resides in the local Philpot Museum, along with many more of these priceless treasures, collected by Mary and others.

Now, fossil hunters were spread out along the beach, using hammers to try to force the stones to give up their long-ago captured secrets and reveal the ancient life imprisoned inside. Stones take prisoners and keep them for eternity. I threw some stones against a wall, but none would reveal their secrets to me.

This was the weekend of the annual festival. Crowds of people thronged the streets, many in weird and wonderful costumes. The sound of a band playing in the distance could be heard above the melee. Five girls, identically dressed in pale blue uniforms, dashed past one by one and went through a door into a cabin. I wondered if I'd missed the white rabbit.

Earlier, there had been a procession through the town, with the band leading children in fancy dress. The five girls were part of the band. The announcer's voice boomed out from speakers along the promenade. "The band have had some success recently, last year, or, er, was it the year before, when they were invited to play in America, or, er, was it Canada. Anyway, we're very proud of them. And now, the Flintstones!"

On the beach, an enthralled group of children watched a Punch and Judy show. Just alongside, an evangelist was informing another group that the end was nigh. They didn't seem too concerned.

I wandered to the Cobb, a huge stone construction jutting out into the sea and protecting the harbour. Trapped in these massive stones can be seen the remains of many creatures, fossilised long ago. With surfaces as smooth and reflective as glass, they resemble works of art.

The Cobb at Lyme Regis

Beyond the Misty Fells

Walking along the top level above me was a young couple. I overheard a woman saying, "Oh look, this is where Meryl Streep stood in the film." Her partner replied, somewhat scathingly, "It wasn't her, it was a stuntman!" The stones kept quiet.

As I walked back towards the town, I heard a voice shouting "No!" and crying. I looked to my left, to see a tiny girl, brightly dressed in a pink princess costume, blond ringlets tumbling to her shoulders, stamping her foot on the floor as she cried "No!" yet again.

On the beach stood a large marquee, inviting people in to examine a selection of precious stones and jewels. There might be one for me in there, but, if there was, I couldn't afford it.

A row of deckchairs lined the promenade, all occupied. I carried on walking and was surprised to see a bright yellow tennis ball floating through the air. It bounced on top of a bald man's head and carried on towards the beach. No-one appeared to claim it, and it was soon lost amongst the stones. Another man was holding a bag of chips, and, as he looked away, a seagull darted in and stole one.

The town had shops selling stones. I looked to see if one would somehow make itself known to me, but none did. I felt sorry for these sad, captive stones, many sliced open to reveal their true colours. "Don't worry," I mentally communicated to these stones, "your person will come".

As I made my way to the car park, I felt a sharp pain under my foot. A stone had jumped into my sandal.

I kicked it away.

10

Travails of a guide for the blind

by Jean Gallagher

A chance remark at a social function persuaded me to follow up an invitation to train as a sighted guide for the blind. I duly presented myself for interview at a quiet house in a residential area of Bolton with about two dozen other people from the North of England. It was not a formal interview, more a social gathering, although I remember having quite a serious conversation with a young woman who turned out to be one of the selection committee.

It had been a pleasant day out, and I did not think much more about it until I got a phone call a few days later inviting me to attend for training. I made another trip to the same address, but the atmosphere was very different. I had hardly gone two steps into the reception room when I was greeted by a charming girl who introduced herself as my guide for the day and gave me dark glasses, which she fixed securely, tying them at the back of my head so that I could not see anything.

What a shock! Suddenly, I felt completely blind myself – and extremely vulnerable. She let me hold her arm and feel my way to a door: hard – try it yourself; even in a familiar room, it is not easy. The, by now, large group – all new trainees with sighted guides – were assembled in what seemed like a large room, where, for an hour, we were made to experience what it was like to be blind. Then it was lunchtime. Again, the tortuous path to the dining room, feeling our way carefully, upstairs, downstairs, feeling for a door, a chair, a table and the satisfaction when we were finally seated and feeling for a knife and fork.

I had got over the first shock by now and started to think what a good training this was going to be – one was getting oneself into the mind of a blind person. And so it went on. After six months, I was invited to join a small group in York and travelled nervously to a hotel. Brenda had been chosen as my first client. We were to share a twin-bedded room. When I had checked in and found the bedroom, here she was, making a cup of tea as well as I could have done myself. Brenda, smart and fortyish, had been blinded at nine. She had been wheeling a friend's baby in a high perambulator which toppled over, hitting her in her face and damaging her eyes.

We bonded well, and the group of ten people, five guides and five clients, had a very enjoyable weekend. We visited the cathedral, walked the walls of the city and did a full tour of the Viking Centre as well as enjoying delicious meals with lively conversations. The five clients had all been blinded by accidents of various kinds.

They were a wonderful group of people. One could not help but be impressed by their courage in adjusting to such tragedies. There was no self-pity. Two of them had university degrees and now worked in universities as teachers. On this holiday weekend, we, the guides, were the eyes of the group, using the skills we had been taught to describe for them all the details of the places which we visited, the meals we ate, the colours of everything around us, and, of course, guiding them through any difficulties. For me, this was the start of some memorable trips around the world.

One outstanding trip was to Eilat in Israel. I was excited about this trip because one of the planned visits, to Petra, the Rose Red City, had long been a dream of mine.

Beyond the Misty Fells

We set off as planned, and the journey passed uneventfully. When the E1A1757 made its descent, I was surprised how different it was from what I had expected. As well as sand, there were great outcrops of rock, and, as we disembarked, we were met with a blast of hot air. The bureaucracy at Heathrow had been something, but now there was a change. The questioning was much tougher, and the people had a kind of arrogance about them that had not been evident in London. The presence of firearms was not only more noticeable but very disturbing.

Leaving the airport, we made a 45-minute bus ride to our destination, the Lagoona Hotel, and quickly settled into our rooms. From the outset, I was impressed with the hotel. Some of us took our first walk into town, our initial impressions being of a very new and upmarket resort. Time passed quickly, and, by 5 o'clock, darkness had fallen. We retired to our rooms to get ready for dinner. It was a surprise to find that it was strictly kosher. However, before us was an extensive display of food, the hotel policy being 'eat as much as you like', which we all did.

Six o'clock on the following morning saw us on our way to the ancient city of Petra in Jordan. After a short coach ride, we stopped at the Israeli border and, once more, found ourselves in the midst of a bureaucratic nightmare. The crossing into Jordan took nearly two hours. We soon became aware of the difference between the two countries: it was as though we had stepped back about 100 years in time. Our first stop was at the well of Moses. Then, the coach stopped again, this time at an Arab market, where many of us bought Arab head-dresses as a shield from the blazing sun. The heat was intense, in the low nineties with no shade. It was as we were approaching the Siq, the narrow ravine which leads one down to the hidden city of Petra, that two of us got separated from the rest of the party. I had been assigned to look after

Lorraine. She was a gorgeous blonde, slim, sylphlike – and completely blind.

We had all been advised to drink four litres of water a day, essential to prevent dehydration. Lorraine had ignored this advice and was consequently very ill. She was vomiting and had a high temperature. That's when I realised that my dream of visiting the long-lost rose-red city of Petra was at an end. My responsibility as a sighted guide was to look after her, and, to the best of my ability, this is what I did. It was a nightmare. I negotiated the hire of two horses and, fortunately, found some water and shade. It was there, when we waited to be collected for the return journey, that she told me the story of her life. She was born blind. Her mother died at her birth, and she was brought up by an elderly father. Eventually, she became a prostitute. After a broken love affair, her father suggested she come on this holiday to recover. Poor girl, she was so unhappy.

I was asked to stay with her for the rest of the week, which meant that I missed another longed-for trip, to Masada and the Dead Sea. Instead, I enjoyed the hotel's facilities, including the pool.

On the last day of our holiday, with the falling of darkness came the start of the Jewish Sabbath. The dining room was filled with candles, and people were noticeably quieter – that is until nightfall. That weekend was the 50th anniversary of the foundation of the state of Israel. In the evening, the dining room became alive. Since we were British, we were advised to keep a low profile. We were ushered into a side room just as a procession was passing along the hallway into the dining room.

The pageantry was astounding. Quite unused to Jewish ceremony, we were absolutely astonished at the elaborate clothing worn by both men and women. The dresses dripped with jewels, the head dresses were elaborate, and the silent tread of the feet made the atmosphere eerie.

Looking back on this trip after 17 years, I feel a deep sadness that the troubles of the region have worsened. A truly beautiful country, full of ancient history, has been unable to find the peace and security for its people that it set out to accomplish with such high ideals. I am no longer a guide for the blind. Age and other problems limit me these days, but I feel very privileged to have experienced these historical sights with such brave, talented blind people.

11

Danglers, discontinuity and discombobulation

by Anna Nolan

This chapter combines three skits which are a re-make of the humorous sketches originally posted on Anna's blog, *Flaming English.* The sentences she is poking fun at, which are entirely authentic, come from her vast archives of common language lapses, accumulated over decades of assiduous linguistic research.

The medical miracle

"Blimey, your health service ... it's called the NHS, isn't it?"

"Yep, the National Health Service – second to none."

"It must be."

"Glad you think so."

"I do, I do: the mind boggles."

"Well, I wouldn't go quite so far ..."

"But it's extraordinary!"

"What exactly?"

"Your midwifery – amazeballs!"

"How do you mean?"

"Delivering babies."

"What's so amazing about delivering babies?"

"Well, it isn't usually a walk in the park – not in Poland anyway."

"I'd say not *anywhere.*"

"A-a-a-a, but that's just it."

"That's just *what?*"

"It is, apparently."

"It is *what?*"

"A walk in the park."

"Look, you are not making any sense here – *what* is a walk in the park?"

"How you deliver babies. In Britain."

"Get away!"

"No, no, it is."

"Says who?"

"The Times Educational Supplement. I've found this article – in your archives. Listen to this."

> When delivered in a fresh, artistic way, children will seize on writing as they do art and drawing.

"Oh this, ha, ha, ha!"

"What's so funny? I mean what a feat: they manage to deliver kids in a fresh way. *And* artistic! I defy you to beat that."

"No, no, they don't deliver *children!*"

"What do you mean they don't deliver children? Are you saying that *The Times Educational Supplement* would have wilfully misinformed its readers?"

"No, no, of course not; it's just that they obviously didn't know their grammar."

"Are you saying you need to know grammar to deliver babies?"

"No, yes ... I mean *no!* Well, everybody needs grammar to communicate – grammar is the mortar that holds the bricks of vocabulary together – but this has nothing to do with babies; it's a dangler."

"A dangling baby?"

"NOT A BABY – THERE IS NO BABY – IT'S A DANGLING PARTICIPLE!!!"

"A dangling *what?*"

"Participle. In this context, 'delivered' is a dangling participle."

"But why is it dangling?"

"Because they made it refer to the wrong noun."

"The Times Educational Supplement did?"

"They did. They obviously thought that you could relate an initial participle such as 'delivered' to the object – which, in this sentence, is 'writing' – but you can't."

"You can't?"

"Nope. Initial participles will always be interpreted as referring to *the subject* of the main clause – *ALWAYS*. And the subject here is 'children'*.*"

"Sure, it's an important subject."

"No, no, I don't mean a subject of discussion – I mean grammar. It's a very common error."

"It is?"

"Yep. But it's very easy to put right. Whenever an initial participle is meant to refer to the object instead of the subject, you just change the voice of the main clause from active to passive – that's all."

"Is that *really* all?"

"Yep. Because, when you change the voice, the object becomes the subject."

"And what happens to the subject?"

"It becomes the agent."

"Secret?"

"Get away! Look, what they were trying to say was this."

When delivered in a fresh, artistic way, *writing* will be seized on by children as eagerly as art and drawing.

"Is that *really* what they were trying to say?"

"Absolutely. It would be better to use 'taught' instead of 'deliver', though, but they have this obsession with *delivering* everything – it's officialese."

"Official *WHAT?*"

"Official*ese – jargon.*"

"In *Britain?*"

"Yep."

"Blow me down!"

Challenge for teachers and taxmen

"This standard-of-living crisis that people keep on about here."

"Yes?"

"Is it really *that* bad?"

"So they say."

"It's scary: I didn't think that even *professionals* would suffer."

"Actually, professionals are not doing too badly, all things considered."

"But that's not what they are implying."

"Who?"

"The Times Educational Supplement."

"Why? What have they written?"

"This."

First, we could ensure that all schools employ more teachers, especially those in challenging circumstances.

"No, no, it's discontinuity."

"What are they going to discontinue?"

"Nothing, nothing: discontinuity is short for *discontinuous modification*."

"What's that when it's at home?"

"When the phrase being modified is separated from the phrase, or clause, modifying it."

"A-a-a-a, you mean like … when you have … when it's … what do you mean *exactly?*"

"Just look at your sentence; what they should have written is this."

First, we could ensure that *all schools, especially those in challenging circumstances,* employ more teachers.

"That's better."

"Yep. Discontinuity is actually very common, and some of it can be quite funny. It's just that the authors don't seem to notice."

"They don't notice?"

"Nope. Listen to this – from *The Independent.*"

I had a water leak into the kitchen from the flat above, which required redecoration.

"The flat *above?* Why on earth would the flat *above* require redecoration?"

"It wouldn't: they meant the flat *below.*"

"So why didn't they say so?"

"Why do you think?"

"Because they didn't twig what they were actually saying – with this … this dis … dis …"

"Continuity – *discontinuity.* Spot on. So how would you amend this nonsense?"

"You'd need to put the two bits next to each other."

"What bits?"

"The ones that go together; like this."

I had a water leak from the flat above into *the kitchen, which required redecoration.*

"Absolutely!"

"Imagine a Pole getting one over on a British newspaper!"

"Easily."

"But you said that this *Independent* was quality, didn't you?"

"Not when it comes up with stuff like this, it isn't. And what do you reckon about this one – from *The Sunday Times*?"

City bonuses dodge taxman in Turkish lira.

"Easy-peasy."

City *bonuses in Turkish lira* dodge taxman.

"By Jove, you got it! Wish those hacks would."

Strange but true

"They say reading broadens the mind, don't they?"

"I thought it was travel."

"Oh yes, yes, but reading is also awfully good for one, isn't it?"

"Obviously: without it, there wouldn't … you couldn't … it would be … I mean you would be completely stuffed."

"Absolutely. I have been going through your files: all the newspaper and magazine cuttings you've got there – amazeballs!"

"Yep, I'm a bit of an addict."

"They say the British press is a cut above the rest, don't they?"

"They do, they do. So how did you get on with the stuff?"

"Very educational; it's just that … that I'm not entirely sure about their grasp of geography …"

"You are not?"

"No; take this *Sunday Times* for example*.*"

"What about it?"

"That's what they came up with."

A recent poll of Bloomberg subscribers found Britain has dropped behind Singapore into third place as the city most likely to be the best financial hub two years from now.

"Ha, ha, ha! They've kept me diverted for many years."

"Diverted from *what?*"

"No, no, I mean entertained."

"I can imagine. But honestly – there is a limit!"

"Not necessarily – you wouldn't believe the howlers I've come across."

"Geographical ones?"

"*All* sorts, but I do remember another good geographical one. Listen to this."

Every country has risks of inter-ethnic violence – from Syria to Stockholm.

"Good grief! Where is it from?"

"From *The Sunday Times.*"

"*Another* one?"

"Yep, geography is definitely not their strongest suit, ha, ha, ha!"

"You can say that again, but it looks as though it's not just geography."

"What makes you say that?"

"Because I've found something else."

"What doesn't that surprise me?"

"No, no, honestly, their maths – it' also quite, quite … wonky."

"Wonky? How do you mean?"

"Listen to this."

The survey reveals that two-thirds of British children have televisions in their bedrooms, double the proportion for most of Europe. By contrast, only three-quarters of British children have a shelf of books in their bedrooms.

"Just a sec, just a sec: two-thirds is … is …"

"66.6%."

"And three-quarters is …"

"75%."

"Ha, ha, ha, quite a survey! But I have to say that, on the whole, British journalists are quite good with fractions and percentages."

"Well, obviously not those on *The Rambler.*"

"What did you find?"

"This."

But at this point a mere three percent of routes had been reopened, leaving four out of five paths still shut.

"Just a sec, just a sec: four out of five is … is …"

"80%."

"So it is! I wonder what happened to the remaining 17% of the routes."

"God only knows."

"I think you might well be right!"

12

Lessons learnt

by Victoria Bowmer

In the half light of the approaching dawn, it was difficult to make out the shape of the kayaks lying on the beach. Had it not been for the long-legged girl dressed in the ubiquitous Aussie uniform of shorts and t-shirt waving at us, it would have been easy to walk past them. How did she know we were her clients? It was a safe bet, as we were the only other people on the beach at 5 am.

Sometimes, you simply put your trust in a total stranger, especially when on holiday and filled with a rosy optimism about life, and that is what we did. We were spending a week at Palm Cove in Northern Queensland and, having the previous evening dropped into a random bar for a night cap, found ourselves chatting to an equally random woman who lived locally. We must not, she said, miss out on the best experience in Palm Cove, which happened to be run by her friend. Before we had time to debate the issue, she pulled a mobile phone from her pocket and made the necessary arrangements. It was agreed that her mystery friend would phone us at 4 am to confirm if the weather and sea were suitable, and, if so, we would meet her on the beach before sunrise.

As four more sleepy people emerged from the gloom to join our group, the phenomenally cheery Jenny tossed us buoyancy aids and paddles and pushed us and our kayaks out onto the inky blue ocean. Leaping into her own kayak and speedily joining us, she gave us a few tips on steering and paddling, and off we went. Steering proved to be easy even for novices like ourselves, as following instructions to paddle in the general direction of the vast horizon allowed both for a large degree of error and for space to rectify it. As we left the beach with its gently breaking waves behind us, all we could hear was the light splash of our paddles dipping in and out of the water while our eyes strained over the sea on the lookout for turtle shells breaking the surface. Surprisingly quickly, we as a group began to acclimatise to this new environment, and there was neither need nor desire to break the spell with conversation.

So slowly that it seemed like a trick of the eye, the distant sky began to lighten. Following Jenny's lead, we stopped paddling and sat motionless, a small cluster of insignificant vulnerable blobs on an endless ocean as the rising sun peeped at us over the horizon. As if by magic, the surface of the sea began to sparkle, and, as the disc of the sun rose majestically higher, the salt dried on our legs, and our skin began to prickle with the heat. Who would have thought to apply sun screen in the dark? Not us.

Now that we could see where we were, it was too late to have reservations as to the depth of the ocean, the possibility of sharks and the long, long way back to the beach. Instead of instructing us to turn our kayaks and head straight back to the beach, Jenny confidently led us towards a private island, not surprisingly owned by a friend of hers. Indicating that we should pull our kayaks up onto the beach, she delved into hers and pulled out a bottle of champagne and a tub of fresh strawberries. Wading through the shallow waters sipping our drinks and guzzling the ripe fruit while tiny multi-coloured reef fish nibbled our toes was an unusual start to yet another day in paradise.

Alas, all good things come to an end, and it was an easy paddle back to Palm Cove, which was now buzzing with beach joggers and tourists sauntering by cafes deciding where to have breakfast. Having worked up a healthy appetite, we decided to do the same and chose a cafe not because of its enticing menu but because there was an empty table shaded by an elegant tree that would save our skin from burning further.

Breakfasting at another waterside café three days later, this time by Sydney harbour, we came across a small article deep inside the complimentary newspaper. The headline read, 'Tourists die at Palm Cove'. We avidly read on: had it been a shark attack, a spider bite or, possibly, an early-morning kayaker drowning? It was none of those. Quite simply, a tree at a beach cafe had fallen on a breakfasting couple sitting at the table beneath it. We recognised the name of the cafe and remembered the tree.

We learnt some important lessons on our holiday in Palm Cove: say yes to opportunity, be open to the advice of strangers and live every day as though it were your last.

13   From misty fells *by Aline Hopkins*

From misty fells we journeyed
Through time and space and place,
No thought of what may lie ahead,
What perils we might face.

From misty fells we set our sails,
Crossed oceans wide, made our travails
On paths well trod, in forests green,
Our goal, our quest, those sights unseen.

From misty fells we sallied forth
To deserts red and glaciers white,
East and west, south and north
To catch the dawn, such stunning light.

From misty fells to places far,
Some familiar, some bizarre,
We wandered to the waters blue
With green and gold and turquoise hue.

From misty fells and ghostly meres,
Await us all who dare to go
The wonders of this spinning sphere.
So go, young friend, that you may know

Those misty fells and towering spires,
The dreaming days and night-time fires.
At journey's end we will recall
The thrills, the friends, the world, it all.

14

The ups and downs of an Indian experience

by Christine Mitchell

It was the weekend of Diana's wedding to Prince Charles. Having travelled from my home village in Wiltshire, I slept, or tried to, on the floor of Heathrow's terminal 5, listening to the pinging of game machines. Dawn brought the check-in and an endless wait before the Delhi flight was called.

The journey was full of delays and took 26 hours. We were meant to take a flight to Srinagar in Kashmir and an onward flight from there to Leh, but, because of the delays, we missed our connections and took rooms in a Delhi hotel.

Srinagar was beautiful. High mountains surrounded Dal Lake, around which were moored houseboats, where we were to stay overnight. Each houseboat accommodated three guests. There were exquisite exotic carvings of vegetation and flowers inside and out, but the interior furnishings were completely western. We had a houseboat man to clean, a cook who monopolised the kitchen and a shikira boy to take us out onto the lake. It was the Raj and present-day India rolled into one, and we spent a relaxing two days being memsahibs and sahibs.

Meanwhile, our tour representative, a man wearing a smart suit and carrying a briefcase full of money necessary to grease the relevant palms, arranged alternative transport to Leh. But, by then, we were more concerned about the volcanic disturbances in our stomachs. Next day, an open-topped army lorry took us over the highest road pass in the world. For two days, we travelled on a winding single-file dirt track in an army convoy, the pass being, at that time, on the cease-fire line between India and Pakistan.

In Leh, our accommodation was on the floor of the houses belonging to local Ladkhi guides. Leh lies at 12,000 feet, so we stayed for two days to acclimatise, and I found a shop selling what was to be the most important item for the rest of my journey – kaolin and morphine.

Then we started the trek, joining our guides with their loaded pack ponies. In our rucksacks, we carried daily essentials, most especially water, but I was only part-way up the first pass when I collapsed. I was advised to breathe more deeply and slowly and to grab hold of the tail of one of the donkeys so that it could drag me over the pass.

On the trek

Ours was one of the first treks in Ladkhi – it had previously been closed to visitors – and the Ladkhis had no knowledge of altitude sickness. There were, therefore, no facilities for turning back. That night, when we set up camp, the guides prepared our meal of tinned spam and chapattis.

The next day was easier. We were on the Silk Road, at a lower altitude, and passed huge pits dug for bears and wolves. Occasionally, we would see Buddhist temples and gompas, which were shrines set up to dead priests. Alongside these gompas were mani walls, which were about five feet high and some twenty yards long, made up of large flat river stones. The stones had been placed there, over the centuries, by pilgrims and merchants. We were told that we should always pass by the gompas widdershins, this being a long understood mark of respect.

Gompas and mani walls

Beyond the Misty Fells

That night, we camped under some trees near the river Indus. The guides were shy of joining us at mealtimes, although we shared our supplies with them. As usual, they sat around a fire talking, and some locals joined them. One thing they were short of was food containers, so we gave them our big empty spam tins. They reciprocated by returning the tins filled with home-made yoghurt complete with yak hairs.

Before breaking camp next day, we had our usual breakfast of chapattis with Bovril. Our fellow American trekkers thought this was terrible British food, but they soon began to appreciate, and even enjoy, it.

We continued our trek, following the Indus valley. The Indus is a fast-running river fed by the snow melt from the mountains, and we had to cross it. We took off our boots and socks and linked hands. The water was freezing, and we had to rest, dry off and wash our arms and faces on the other side. I noticed that my hands, arms and the rest of my body seemed to be blown up, and I looked like the Michelin man.

That night, we stayed at one of the guides' houses. It was hundreds of years old and built of mud brick with a flat roof. The ground floor housed the animals; the next contained the cooking area and had a hole through to the roof. With the heat coming from the animals and the cooking fire, the house was reasonably comfortable. On the roof were covered rooms with raised shelves made of baked clay, on which we slept. Also on the roof were a shrine and scrolls. The travelling priest had arrived and was chanting from the scrolls.

The following day, we started to climb again. The fields by the Indus are used for growing food and winter feed for the animals. By a track, we met some of the Ladkhi women, hand spinning as they walked with their flocks to find fodder. The women were wearing all the clothes they possessed, even in summer. They had tall head-dresses made of turquoise beads and semi-precious stones. They asked me to have a go at hand spinning, and I tried but had trouble keeping hold of the spindle. The women thought this hilarious. We joined in their laughter and passed round sweets, a special treat for them.

Ladakh women spinning

The next day, I woke up with a nose bleed that would not stop. I dared not move out of my tent but was advised to pinch my nose and carry on with the trek. The nose bleed did not stop until lunchtime.

After a bad night with headaches and continuing stomach problems, the next day was the most difficult. We were still climbing. I could walk only ten slow steps before having to sit down and gasp for breath. I must have fallen an hour behind the others. At the end of the day, we had reached 20,000 feet, the highest point of the trek. The night was a blur, but the good news was that, from now on, we were descending. First, though, there was the Indus to cross again. Bob from Scotland and I were carried across by our guides, who thought it was very funny and laughed at our predicament.

Eventually, we walked down to a monastery with its massive prayer wheels. I turned them all, in thanks for a safe return. There was a bus waiting for us, ready to drive us back to Leh. I used the day there profitably stocking up on more kaolin and morphine. We thanked our guides profusely and gave them presents. I wish I'd known to bring more socks and soap, which seemed most useful to them.

The two-day journey to Srinagar seemed almost relaxing. What a relief to shower and sleep in a proper bed at Lake Dal's reasonable altitude. The day after our arrival, we hired a shikira boy to ferry us about. The locals were washing in the lake, but seeing some dead cats and dogs floating, we decided that swimming was a treat we could miss.

Dal Lake vegetable market

Next day, we arranged for our shikira boy to pick us up before dawn. Part of the lake was used locally for growing vegetables, and, every morning at dawn, the growers would set out to trade these vegetables from their small, overloaded boats. Throughout the trading, there were boys in boats shouting, "Lotus flower for madam". It was noisy and colourful – a unique experience.

Relaxing in a shikira with a friend

That afternoon, we went around Srinagar. Although the town is in India, it is administered by the majority Moslem community. It was noticeable that the Hindu area was poorer than the Moslem one, and we were told that there were frequent disputes between the sects, especially on religious festival days.

We left the next day – this time, by plane from Srinagar and then straight onto our return flight with Japanese airlines. Our journey home, though long, passed without incident.

At home, my GP, who happened to be an ex-army doctor, said, "Coming from India, it's bound to be something exotic." He sent away a sample to a tropical medicine centre and asked me to call back at the weekend. When I returned, he greeted me from the far end of the very long entrance hall saying, "That's your medicine on the table, and you're highly contagious." At least, I didn't have to take kaolin and morphine again.

Later on, those of us who had been on the trek together held a reunion, where we all agreed that it was a privilege to have been able to experience such a wonderful part of the world and that the downs of the trek were far outweighed by the ups: the mountain and desert scenery, the monasteries, Dal Lake, Srinagar and the Ladkhi people.

15

The medium

by Gill Frances

(This is a scene from a play based on a true story. The names have been changed.)

Scene: a 'wartime' kitchen. The sisters Susan and Ellie enter. Susan has been to visit a medium because she is desperate to know if her husband, a POW in Japan, is still alive.

Susan: No, it wasn't how I thought it would be at all. I thought it'd be dark, you know, and sort of mysterious.

Ellie: How was it then? Did she not have a crystal ball?

Susan: I didn't see one. I didn't see anything, really. Just a table and chairs like we have at home. And she made me a cup of tea. Oh, look, Maureen's left her writing book behind. She'll be upset.

Ellie: So did you not find anything out? What did she say?

Susan: *(Takes off her coat.)* She said he was still alive. (*Slowly*) She said she was sure.

Ellie: But how did she know? I mean, she couldn't really know, could she?

Susan: She said I had to bring something of his that he'd worn or handled a lot, so I took that green shirt. The one his mother gave him. And an old handkerchief. And I showed them to her.

Ellie: *(Plumps herself down onto a chair.)* And then what? Is that when she said he was alive?

Susan: No. She told me to sit down, and she made some tea. (*Moves the kettle to the hob and reaches for two unmatched cups.*) And then she asked about the girls. And then she asked how Arthur and me had met and where we courted and where we were married and when the children were born.

Ellie: Oh my God, what did you tell her?

Susan: I don't know. I said about going to the pictures in Gidler Lane. I said my mother wouldn't let Arthur into the house when she found out he voted Conservative.

Ellie: I can't believe you married a dyed-in-the-wool Tory.

Susan: Neither can I, really. (*Laughs.*) But, you know, we didn't talk about politics much when we were courting. (*Measures tea into the pot. Pours on the water.*)

Ellie: And then did she say he was alive?

Susan: No, not right away. She wanted to know how long it was since he'd been posted abroad and whether I'd had any letters.

Ellie: Eh, Susie, *(giggling)* she might have been a spy. Did she have a German accent or anything?

Susan: She sounded like us, Ellie. (*Goes to the pantry door for sterilised milk.*) I've got nothing to go with the tea.

Ellie: I've got me ciggies, and Jack's taking me out later. (*Lights up.*) What happened after that?

Susan: She picked up the shirt and sort of stroked it a couple of times. I thought she looked like she was in a trance. I felt really awkward. I must have fidgeted or something because she looked up at me and she said, "Oh, sorry, I forgot you were there for a minute. He's alive. This doesn't belong to anyone on the other side."

Ellie: Sounds sure of herself.

Susan: Yes. (*Pours the tea. Adds a small amount of milk. Then, with a change of expression.*) Oh, what would you have with this if you could have anything in the world, Ellie? I'd have crumpets. With lots of butter. I'd have so much butter it would drip down my fingers (*mimes it*), and I'd have to rush for a cloth to wipe it up, and I wouldn't have to worry about making it last or save it all to give to the girls. (*Pours tea. Hands over a cup.*) Here. And I'd have raspberry jam.

Ellie: I'd rather have a fag. (*Raises her cup.*) Mind you, I'd rather have a port and lemon as well if it comes to that. I might get one tonight, too. Jack likes taking me to the pub.

Susan: How long have you been going out? Does Mother know? Does she mind taking care of Mollie?

Ellie: Mother knows everything, and what difference will it make to her if she takes care of one more? It's been six weeks now.

Susan: Any chocolates? Any silk stockings? (*Laughs.*)

Ellie: Don't be so soft. (*Holds up a scarf.*) He did pass me this scarf of his to keep me warm, though, the other night. What do you think, our Sue? Is it a good omen?

Susan: (*Takes the scarf and strokes it. Frowns. Looks abstracted. Gives it back quickly.*) I don't know, Ellie. I don't think I have the gift.

Ellie: Try not to worry, Sue. You know Arthur. If anyone can come through this, he will.

16

Travels in the Middle East

by Rowland Bowker

Rowland Bowker looks back over 50 years to the time he spent travelling and working in Turkey, when conditions were very different from today's.

My experience of the Middle East spans almost 50 years, from 1955 to 2000. In 1955 and 1956, I worked as a teacher in Ankara, Turkey. My students were sons of the rich. Even then, it was thought that being able to speak English gave one a great advantage, and I taught English and science.

For Christmas 1955, three of us travelled to Jerusalem. In those days, East Jerusalem and Bethlehem were in Jordan. The overland journey to Jerusalem and back through Turkey, Syria, Lebanon and Jordan took four days. There was no trouble in Lebanon then: Beirut was the Paris of the Middle East and a leave destination greatly favoured by ex-pats working in the area.

During the summer of 1955, there had been no rain, which resulted in a water shortage. As water was turned on only between midnight and 2 am, one had to set the alarm clock for midnight and fill up the bath. To save electricity, the voltage was reduced at about 8 pm every day, so radios would not work after that time.

Beyond the Misty Fells

Coffee does not grow in Turkey, nor does tea, so supplies ran out, but, while I was there, alcoholic drinks were always available. Local wine, vodka and liqueurs were both plentiful and cheap.

Bus travel was very unreliable. Since new tyres were unobtainable, it was usual to see vehicles driven with great holes in their tyres wrapped round with cloth. Breakdowns were common, too: it was quite possible for a bus journey scheduled to take 12 hours to last 36. Travel by DOLMUS was slightly better – five people were squeezed into one car. Perhaps you know that DOLMUS means stuffed . . .

With five or six beds to a room, Turkish hotels outside the main cities were quite an experience. We discovered that the lights were left on all night – not for security reasons, but to make the bed bugs less active. Sheets were changed about once a month.

Despite these minor problems, I enjoyed my year in Turkey. I found Turks very friendly, although I did not like my job very much because the children were badly behaved. It was the custom to report a badly behaved boy to the Bashi, who took him to the bathroom, where he was beaten. This system did not apply to the girls, who were given separate instruction. The lack of school discipline led to most students taking private lessons from us. This meant that my salary was about three or four times what I would have earned in the UK.

I have concentrated on the 'bad' things so far, but, in fact, the good things far outweighed them. The people were unfailingly hospitable, although it took a little while to get used to the Turkish men's habit of walking hand in hand. The food was delicious, especially the sweets such as baklava and delicate creamy yoghurt.

Yes, I did enjoy my year in Turkey and go back there on holiday as often as I can.

17

Travels in the Far East

by Rowland Bowker

Rowland Bowker remembers a trip on the Trans-Siberian Railway in 1985.

It was necessary to choose the correct time of year to undertake this journey. In winter, temperatures could be down to between minus 30 and minus 40 degrees centigrade. In summer, they could be 40 degrees or more, so the obvious times to travel are spring or autumn. I took this trip in early October 1985 with a group of ten people.

We started from London with a champagne breakfast, which I did not enjoy very much. I don't like alcohol early in the morning, and I don't like champagne! Vodka would have been more acceptable.

The first unusual event was the changing of the bogies on the train at the frontier between Poland and Russia. This took about two hours and occurred between one o'clock and three o'clock in the morning, coinciding with a customs inspection. We had been warned not to attempt to take into the Soviet Union anything even vaguely pornographic, and I suddenly realised that the book I had brought with me was Chaucer's *Canterbury Tales*. The customs officer arrived and started to look at the literature we were carrying. He picked up the *Canterbury Tales* and studied it for about half an hour before handing it back to me with a smile.

Beyond the Misty Fells

We broke the journey at Moscow and spent three nights in the city. It was a relief to get out of the train because everybody smoked, even though it was forbidden and even though all the windows were screwed shut – some of the passengers in the sleepers smoked up to a hundred cigarettes a day. In 1985, the Soviet Union was short of everything except vodka, and the hotel in Moscow allowed only half a cup of coffee with breakfast.

The next stop was Irkutsk, about four days away. The temperature was below zero, but we made a day trip to Lake Baikal, which I remembered from my days studying oceanography at Liverpool University. The professor had mentioned the *seiches* – a *seiche* is when the whole mass of water moves back and forth – to be observed on this lake. From Irkutsk, it wasn't far to the border with Mongolia, and it was noticeable that there was more in the shops in the capital, Ulan Bator, than there had been in the Soviet Union. To our surprise, there was an even greater variety of things for sale in the shops in China.

After three days in Beijing doing the standard tours, we embarked on the last part of our voyage, a 36-hour journey by train to Gwanjou, previously known as Canton. The Trans-Siberian Railway was now just a memory. After three days in Gwanjou, the train journey to Hong Kong seemed both short and pleasant, and, indeed, at that time many people in Hong Kong would make a visit to China for just one day.

18

My around the world in 80 days

by Aline Hopkins

(If I can do it, anyone can!)

"I'm thinking of going around the world," I said to the travel agent.

"When are you thinking of going?" he asked.

"In about three weeks."

"Ah, well, in that case I'd better clear the decks!"

It all started when my nephew, who lives in New York State, invited me to his engagement party. The death of my mother, followed by endless rain over the previous year, had been getting me down, so I thought I could go – and then keep heading west. Why not?

The engagement party was held at the famous Saratoga Springs Racetrack, which was holding a race meeting and celebrating its 150th anniversary at the same time. The party 'suite' turned out to be a two-storey cabin of sorts, which, unfortunately, was on the bend beyond the finishing line, so the only time the horses ran past was after they'd finished the race. One fainted, and a worrying few minutes was spent while it was hosed down and showered with buckets of water; fortunately, it recovered.

The upstairs deck was open but covered, and, on my way up, I did a double-take as I saw a group of nuns going into the next-door suite. A closer look revealed that the suite was filled with priests and nuns, obviously enjoying a day at the races. "Ask them if they've had any good tips from him upstairs," said my sister, hopefully. Not that she'd actually placed any bets, or was likely to.

The next day, some of us headed up to Canada to enjoy a few days' fishing at a very peaceful lakeside spot. The fish were biting, the loons were singing, and the weather was good.

The first stop on my agenda after saying goodbye to my relatives was Chicago, the windy city. My reason for stopping here was to see an exhibition at the History Museum, of photographs taken by Vivian Maier. She worked as a nanny most of her life but was also a keen photographer. Virtually every day, she took photographs, which lay undiscovered until storage lockers she rented were sold off after her death. The buyers discovered a wealth of incredible street photography, covering around fifty years of Chicago and US history. It's ironic, quite sad in fact, that her images were not made public when she was alive.

After seeing the exhibition, I had lunch in the museum café. Looking up, I was surprised to see planes doing sky-writing. It turned out to be the weekend of the annual Chicago air show, so I went out and enjoyed the spectacle of aerobatic displays, stunt flying and parachutists, all performing over the lake.

Next day, I flew to Rapid City, a small town, its main claim to fame being the statues of American Presidents on every street corner. From here, I took a trip into Custer State Park, where herds of bison roam, and, as I watched them ambling down a hill to a watering hole, I felt very guilty at having eaten buffalo burgers the night before. At the nearby Needles range, a viewpoint offered a vast expanse of tree-filled landscape, stretching as far as the eye could see.

© Aline Hopkins

Bison in Custer State Park

In Rapid City, I joined a coach tour which was heading south. First stop was the Mount Rushmore National Monument, where the heads of Roosevelt, Lincoln, Washington and Jefferson stare unendingly over the hordes of tourists who visit this place every day. Not too far away is the even larger Crazy Horse Memorial, still a work in progress, and likely to remain so for many years to come.

Beyond the Misty Fells

The nightly rodeo in Cody provided some skilful entertainment as cowboys and cowgirls of all ages rode, or tried to ride, an assortment of horses, oxen, calves (for the children) and steers and showed their skills with the lasso in timed events. They even rode while a raging thunderstorm passed over the arena.

But it was a toddler wearing a black Stetson who stole the evening when, in the interval, all the children were invited into the arena to take part in games. This small boy in his large cowboy hat staggered around, repeatedly falling over, losing his hat and putting it back on again, oblivious to what the others were doing. The crowd loved him; he was the star of the show.

The star of our show was next on the itinerary – Yellowstone National Park. I sometimes wonder how many people in the world don't know that Yellowstone is a massive super-volcano, which last erupted about 60,000 years ago. A huge reservoir of magma a few miles below the surface is what gives rise to this area's geo-thermal features – boiling mud pools, hot springs, geysers and colourful terraces of travertine leached from the hot water bubbling up from the ground.

Old Faithful, true to its name, erupts a tower of hot water every seventy minutes or so. Nearby, other geysers appeared to be in a constant state of eruption. On a cool morning, the whole area is filled with a steamy mist, fuelled by these numerous geysers dotted about the landscape.

Some people claimed to have seen a bear close to Lake Yellowstone, but all my party saw were a few bison, birds and butterflies.

South of Yellowstone is the hugely impressive mountain range known as The Tetons. Rising up sharply from the surrounding plain, these snow-capped peaks must have seemed an insurmountable barrier to early settlers crossing America. A raft trip down the Snake River offered views of these massive grey peaks, and the banks of the river presented us with bald eagles, ospreys and colourful native flowers.

The Tetons

A long day's drive brought us to Salt Lake City, its light-coloured buildings gleaming in the sunlight. A huge amphitheatre was the setting for the Mormon Tabernacle Choir's weekly live radio broadcast – an interesting performance to watch and listen to, including a repertoire of good old-fashioned favourites like *When the Saints Go Marching in*.

The Salt Lake itself disappointed, though the insect life teeming on its shores attracted an enormous number of gulls and other birds. Nearby was the world's largest copper mine, a vast gash in the mountainside.

It had been good to travel with a varied and interesting group of people. The final dinner was an occasion of mixed emotions, saying goodbye to new-found friends, people who had welcomed this foreigner into their midst with open arms, who had made this trip special and whom I would probably never see again.

Alone once more, I flew to San Francisco and immediately took a trip to Yosemite National Park to seek out the viewpoints made iconic by the famous photographer Ansel Adams. In this wilderness, sheer cliff faces rise up from the valley floor, and, whilst they might look impossible, there were groups of climbers just visible as tiny specks on the face of El Capitan.

The vast bulk of Half Dome, shining brightly but occasionally dappled by shade from clouds overhead, loomed impressively above those of us who rode through the valley floor in the wagons which take tourists around the park.

Because of drought, the famous waterfalls had dried up. A small trickle of water being blown by the wind over Bridal Veil Falls showed how the falls got their name, but in an unimpressive fashion. Fires were raging in various parts of the park, but the valley was untouched. Deer sheltered in the shade, ground squirrels hunted around the car parks, and blue birds flitted through the trees.

I felt dwarfed in Muir Woods, where towering redwoods are preserved, some of them several hundred years old. Later, a boat trip around San Francisco Bay offered good views of the famous Golden Gate Bridge and the notorious Alcatraz prison.

I was surprised to find that my visit coincided with the start of the America's Cup boat race. Huge catamarans, one representing New Zealand and one the USA, were racing one another in the bay. Throngs of people lined the harbour front to get a good view, and it was incredible to watch these massive boats seemingly flying along the surface of the water on what looked like a hockey stick protruding from underneath the boat. Sadly, I saw only the first day of racing, as I headed to Los Angeles the following day to take a flight to my next destination, the Cook Islands.

© Aline Hopkins

The America's Cup taking place in San Francisco

Beyond the Misty Fells

If ever there was a tropical paradise, this is it. I flew to Raratonga and then took a small plane to the atoll of Aitutaki. The large turquoise-coloured lagoon around Aitutaki is bounded by coral reefs and small islands and contains many species of colourful tropical fish. A traditional boat carries visitors out to One Foot Island, where the post office opens for a few hours so that people can have their passports stamped – after, of course, a delicious lunch, a swim in the warm lagoon and a rest under the swaying palm trees on the white sandy beach!

One Foot Island, Aitutaki, the Cook Islands

Beyond the Misty Fells

Back on Raratonga, I took the bus which circles the island clockwise, and then anti-clockwise, each trip taking just forty-five minutes. There isn't really a lot to do on Raratonga for someone who can't swim and doesn't sunbathe. A small, beautiful island; time moves slowly here. Chickens range freely around the streets, scuttling out of the way of motor cycles carrying two or three family members. The colourful Sunday market bustles with people, with the flowers on stalls reflected even more colourfully in the flower patterns on the material on the clothes stalls.

My next stop was Christchurch, New Zealand. The flight from Auckland was over range after range of snow-capped mountains. I knew that Christchurch had had an earthquake in 2011, but nothing had prepared me for the devastation, the total absence of any habitable buildings in the centre of the city. People are resilient, however, and businesses had created a shopping area constructed entirely from shipping containers where once there had been streets and shops.

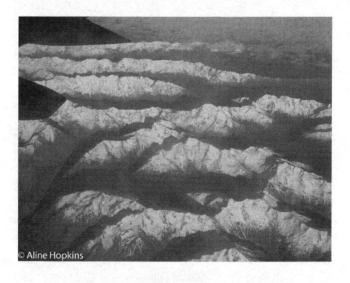

Flying over South Island, New Zealand

Beyond the Misty Fells

It was spring here, and the cherry trees were in full, resplendent bloom. Hiring a car, I headed south down the coast and then turned inland to Lake Tekapo, which is the most unbelievable shade of turquoise-bluey-green. Flanked by snow-covered mountain ranges, this place was truly picturesque. The small Church of the Good Shepherd has an enviable position right on the shore, with a window behind the altar looking directly down the lake.

Further south, there were more lakes of unbelievable hues and incredible views of Mount Cook rising massively in the hazy distance.

From Queenstown, I took a trip to Milford Sound, on a very rainy day, on roads where avalanches had occurred and been cleared, but more looked likely. Visibility in the Sound was intermittent, but the rainfall produced numerous waterfalls, gushing down from the steep-sided, incredibly high walls of this fjord. Boats appeared tiny by comparison, going as close to the waterfalls as they dared in an attempt to get the tourists they carried thoroughly soaked. Sorry, I take that back: to provide them with good photo opportunities.

Heading north again, I stopped at Lake Wanaka, where I discovered that the Haast Pass, which I was due to cross next morning to reach the west coast, was closed – blocked by landslides.

Fortunately, next morning it had re-opened. I drove up with some trepidation and had to stop where a man in work clothes was holding up traffic. "Go when I tell you to, drive slowly, keep going and do as the men over there say" were his instructions. I set off along the track the men had cleared through the massive mudslide, weaving around boulders until I reached the far side. I breathed a sigh of relief. The rest of the pass had other mudslides, but none as big as that one. I later discovered that two people had been washed away, and found dead, a week earlier.

Beyond the Misty Fells

On the west coast, I saw the unusual formations of the Pancake Rocks, visited the Franz Josef glacier and saw kiwis – in captivity, I'm sorry to say. As with all of south island, the scenery as I drove north was fantastic and, at times, utterly breath-taking. When I reached Nelson, on the north coast, the beautiful weather which had been with me since Queenstown finally broke, so I had a rest day before heading south to Kaikoura – *the* place to go whale watching in New Zealand.

I was not disappointed. After half an hour in a catamaran on fairly choppy seas, which, unfortunately, some of my fellow passengers found nauseating, the boat stopped when the sounds of a sperm whale were heard over a microphone lowered into the sea. It surfaced close to the boat and did a few shallow dives, swimming not too far away from us before doing a final big dive, tail flukes full in the air, and that was it. Show over. The captain informed us that the whale then stays underwater for up to forty minutes and that there was no point hanging around waiting for it to surface again. On the way back to the harbour, the boat took a small diversion for people to see seals on the rocks near the shore.

South island appears, in some places, to be over-run with seals. On my way up the west coast, I had seen several colonies, and more on the way south from Nelson. A car park near Kaikoura's south bay had seals lounging around all over the place, with signs everywhere warning people not to get too close. The seals didn't seem too bothered; I didn't see any that weren't fast asleep!

Returning to Christchurch, I noticed that the cherry blossom had faded; it had been a glorious riot of colour flanking the roads when I arrived; now it had gone.

A night flight took me to Sydney, where I was to spend the next week. I was surprised to discover that it was the week of celebrations –

Beyond the Misty Fells

The International Fleet Review – to mark the 100th anniversary of the entry of the first Royal Australian Navy Fleet into Sydney harbour. Consequently, ships of all shapes and sizes from various navies of the world were converging on Sydney, and so were the tall ships – an unexpected bonus. I booked to go on a whale-watching excursion, and, as my boat sailed out of the harbour, the tall ships were lining up to sail in.

It was October, and, at this time of year, humpback whales pass the entrance to Sydney harbour on their annual migration. Luckily, there were several humpback whales passing by that day, and they put on quite a show of breaching, head slapping and tail waving. It was raining, and the guide on the boat said that he thought they liked the feel of the rain on their skin, adding, "You should see them when it's hailing!"

Humpback whale near Sydney

Next day, I took a tour to the Blue Mountains. On a previous visit some years ago, the Three Sisters were hidden by fog, but, on this occasion, the skies were clear, the Sisters were visible, and tourists were everywhere. The area has been developed substantially since my last visit, and now there are viewing platforms, shops and restaurants, and a cable car.

The following day was gloriously sunny, so I decided to go on another whale-watching trip. As we sailed out of the harbour, battleships from Australia, France, Japan and the USA sailed in, with sailors lined up along the decks in true ceremonial fashion. As the boat left the shelter of Sydney harbour, it became clear that the swell was a real problem. People started getting sea-sick, and the Captain announced he was returning to the harbour. At that point, someone announced they had seen a whale blow, so we headed in that direction instead, and even more people got sea-sick. It wasn't long before the Captain took the boat back to the harbour, where we sailed around for a while watching the battleships sail in, greeted by innumerable small sailing boats. Sydney Harbour soon resembled the maritime equivalent of Piccadilly Circus.

The day after that, Prince Harry arrived to take part in the official ceremonies. To escape it all, I took a trip to Port Stephens, where I went on a dolphin-spotting cruise and was rewarded with good views of several groups of dolphins. Even better viewing was to be had at the harbour side, where baby swallows were being fed at regular intervals by their parents, on the wing.

That evening, the celebrations were brought to a close with a magnificent display of fireworks, typically Sydney. What was a surprise was the further firework display at Darling Harbour, apparently a regular Saturday-night event and something I thought we should adopt back home.

A hot and steamy Singapore awaited. This island seems to be in a state of constant redevelopment and construction, and sometimes it's difficult to tell whether a building is being put up or taken down.

Beyond the Misty Fells

For a relatively small island, Singapore offers a great deal to see. Little India and Chinatown are both fascinating and have managed to keep some of the traditional shops and dwellings despite all the work going on around them. Reclaimed land to the south now houses the Gardens by the Bay, where man-made tree structures make for an interesting landscape. The Singapore Flyer (like the London Eye) is a new addition since my last visit, and the Marina Bay Sands hotel, with a boat-shaped structure atop its three towers, dominates the skyline.

One place to go to escape the hustle and bustle is the Botanic Gardens, which houses a superb orchid garden. The hot and humid climate offers perfect conditions for orchids to thrive, and they grow here in abundance. I, on the other hand, don't fare so well in the heat and humidity and was pleased to rest with a cool drink and an ice cream beside a pond covered in giant water lilies.

The metro system in Singapore is one of the cleanest in the world, and I rode on it to the western suburb of Jurong, where there is a very large bird park, housing many of Asia's colourful bird species. Sadly, I couldn't stay there very long, as I had an evening flight to Frankfurt, where I caught a flight to Manchester and, from there, a train home.

I had kept a journal on my trip and, writing up my final day, realised that it was day 80 of my trip. I had been around the world in 80 days, admittedly not overland in the style of Verne's Phileas Fogg and of Michael Palin, but it had still been an amazing adventure.

Was it the trip of a lifetime? Perhaps – until the next one!

19

Jetlagged in Canberra

by Gill Frances

From the Museum terrace, across the lake,
I see cars rising and falling
Over Commonwealth Avenue Bridge.
Images invade my mind of a drive
To Belconnen, and, for a few breaths, I am
In the Suzuki, watching my son
Reach for the volume control, hearing Adele
Scorch her way through *Rumour Has It*.

Rumour has it there's a crocodile in the sky
Where the Milky Way should be. I look up,
Imagine its body, lit with stars, lurching
Through indigo dark
To settle into its aboriginal space
Above a younger, redder Earth.
I blink slowly, remembering the 'roos
In Yarralumla Park this morning,
Gazing at us glumly from the brindle dust.

There is a taste of toasted banana bread in my mouth.
From a nearby pine, a miner bird
Monitors the crumbs on my plate.

Beyond the Misty Fells

How *odd* the birds are here! I think of magpies
Gurgling and fluting from City sycamores,
Cockatoos screeching through scribble gums,
Crimson rosellas *klee-kleeing* in the park.

Two women drink wine at the next table
And talk about the latest exhibition,
Their un-English tones falling and rising.
It comes to me that our grandchildren
Have Aussie accents, too: "*Grendma,*
We're going to a *pardy!*"

A black, bright swan mooches by.
A mile away, Mount Ainslie glimmers
As the wind twists sunlight through a million leaves.
Almost, I smell eucalyptus.

I close my eyes. Realise
I love this place,
Love the way Australia assembles itself,
Piece by piece,
Scene by scene,
In the Dream Time.

20

Taranaki 360

by Victoria Bowmer

I instinctively huddled for shelter behind the bulk of my husband as we scuttled between the terminal building and our plane while ferocious gusts of wind attacked us first from one side then from the other. Not even the prospect of a turbulent flight could pop the bubbles of excitement I was experiencing at the prospect of our journey today.

I love to fly, not for the in-flight entertainment or the dubious food, but for the opportunity to view the natural beauty of our planet from above. I have flown over glaciers, been entranced by icebergs floating in intense blue oceans, crossed frozen continents watching the vague outlines of roads and runways gradually appear as, with the plane travelling southwards, the sun's increasing warmth melted the snow and been amazed by endless brown arid deserts and the jewelled beauty of the Great Barrier Reef. I feel privileged to be able to experience our world from a perspective my grandparents and great-grandparents had never had the opportunity to do.

I was particularly excited about today's flight as, having checked with the airline and questioned my travel agent, I knew with certainty that we were scheduled to fly directly over Mount Taranaki, a 2,518-metre perpetually snow-capped volcano. In anticipation, my binoculars were already swinging from a cord around my neck.

After being held up by a meeting at work, my husband had insisted that, having arrived at the airport with only moments to spare, we should check ourselves in at the self-service desk. Anxiously, I watched over his shoulder to ensure he select me a window seat, and we quickly printed our boarding cards and sprinted to the gate.

If this were a house rather than a plane, even the most unscrupulous estate agent would struggle to describe it as anything other than compact, and, as I scanned the few rows of seats looking for the number on my card, my excitement fizzled away. Instead of a window, I was faced with a solid piece of moulded grey plastic. Our row was alongside the propeller, and, for safety reasons, the window was blanked out.

My husband, who is the first person I turn to in any crisis and to whom I was now bitterly complaining about not having a window seat, appeared to be unconcerned by my disappointment. Having, with a combination of ingenuity and concentration, miraculously folded his long legs into a space the depth of a shoe box, he settled back and opened his newspaper as I began to pack away my binoculars. Suddenly, I became conscious of a polite cough from the gangway and looked across at a diminutive cabin steward. "Excuse me, Madam, I couldn't help but overhear you and have spoken with the captain, who has given me permission to move you to the single empty window seat by the exit at the front." My husband began folding his newspaper and, looking directly into the eyes of the steward, who, although standing, was a similar height, put on his most authoritative office voice, "As I need the legroom, it should be *me* moving to the seat at the front." Without shifting his gaze, the steward politely but firmly replied, "But, Sir, did you also bring your binoculars especially to view Mount Taranaki?"

Settled in my new seat, I was so mesmerised by the chain of lesser volcanoes appearing below me that, at first, I barely registered the voice of our captain making an unscheduled announcement: "On board today, we have a visitor to New Zealand. I have been given permission by air traffic control to deviate from our route to fly a circuit of Mount Taranaki so that she can get a better view of a unique part of our beautiful country."

As the plane banked to the left and the snow-capped peak of Mount Taranaki filled the window, I stretched out my legs and wondered: am I, at this moment, the luckiest person in the world?

21

Magic places

by John Howell

High places drenched in magic lift us from our other selves,
Casting spells that move us to return and drink their potions.
Blue lakes and fjords, snow-filled woods are just as strong –
Yet nature's landscapes do not enchant alone.

Our minds attach some other places with their own force,
Mysteriously emerging from deep thoughts explored.
The spine-tingling memories of sharing hopes and fears
At one spellbound spot, now forever ours.

How many places, near and far, which we have passed,
That left no witchcraft lingering around the memory.
It is hard now to remember where they were or who was there,
But other sites and sights burn into the mind, vivid and everlasting.

Places where we were together, or met a glorious friend.
Places where sparks flew from the stones, the very air alive.
Or when some ray of sunlight, or passing cloud formation
Changed a landscape into a fleeting vision of perfection.

Places where we, adrenaline flooded, were alight,
All senses glowing. Passionately alert to sound, sight and smell.
That shock of contact that brought us together,
Forever leaving that place holding safe our magic.

22

Mixed metaphors and opposite meanings

by Anna Nolan

This chapter combines two skits from Anna's blog, *Flaming English*. Again, all the lambasted sentences are authentic; she maintains that her imagination is woefully unequal to coming up with similar revelations.

Breathing in the hand of history

"A-a-a-a, they've finally blown the lid off it."

"Who did?"

"The British press."

"Blown the lid off *what?*"

"Why reading standards are slipping in this country; you told me they were."

"Regrettably. So what reason did the press give?"

"Well, they haven't actually been *all that* explicit, but one can draw one's own conclusions."

"But what did they say *exactly?*"

"This."

Much better that future generations of children can breathe in and touch the hand of history than read a descriptive narrative in a book.

"Oh this – ha, ha, ha!"

"But it's not funny; I think it's rather sad myself. Then again, breathing in the hand of history is bound to bring at least *some* benefit."

"You can't be serious!"

"But I'm ..."

"No, no, no, they've simply mixed their metaphors."

"They have?"

"Yep. You grow up, you get yourself an education, you become a journalist – and then you come up with such gibberish."

"You do?"

"Yep. Look what I've found in *The Times Educational Supplement.*"

A drop in high achievement among seven-year-olds' basic
skills is swinging the pendulum further towards phonics.

"You mean this drop found itself among skills because it was
swinging on this pendulum so hard?"
"Give me strength – it's just another mindless jumble."
"But, but … what does it actually mean?"
"Not entirely sure but probably something along these lines."

The decline in basic skills among seven-year-olds is swaying
opinion further towards phonics.

"A-a-a-a, that's better. I mean obviously not that your kids are
slipping; I didn't …"
"I know, I know. Look, mixed metaphors are quite common. I have
another one here for you – also from *The Times Educational
Supplement.* It's supposed to be an imploration for British colleges to
resist too much government control."

Otherwise, the ideological bandwagon, supplemented by
battalions of unthinking, unblinking 'change agents' will infect the
terrain.

"Well, you certainly wouldn't want to be infected by a bandwagon;
it could be very unpleasant."
"But not half as unpleasant as reading dross such as this. As for
those unthinking battalions, they seem to have already infected quite a
large terrain of our media – and other institutions."

"Hmmm, I'm beginning to ..."

"Yep, so you should. I think you'll enjoy this one: I found it in *The Sunday Times.*"

The situation demands an intellectual solvent that cuts through the woolly-headed posturing of our make-believe world.

"But ... there's ... what the ... it's, it's ... is this *really* what the situation demands?"

"Nope, I reckon it demands far, *far* more than that. But it's not just the press."

"It isn't?"

"Nope. That's what I've just heard on Radio 4."

This streak of independence is getting its voice.

"Can't you have a streaky voice?"

"Maybe after 10 double vodkas, but this is *not* what they meant."

"Hmmm ..."

"And that's what they said about our dwindling electricity supply."

The cushion between supply [of electricity] and demand has dipped to a 10-year low.

"But the cushions on my sofa are always dipping to the floor."

"Dropping – not dipping. But *this* cushion certainly does neither."

"Wasn't this on Radio 4, though? You said it was ..."

"Yes, yes, quality."

"Blow me down!

Parental negligence and economic ineptitude

"Surely, that's child abuse!"

"What do you mean? Another case of sexual …"

"No, no, no, this one's totally unique."

"It is?"

"It is, it is! I haven't come across anything like this in my entire life!"

"Like what?"

"Like this health advice."

"What health advice?"

"In *The Sunday Times.* To think that a quality newspaper … you said this *Sunday Times* was a quality newspaper, didn't you?"

"I did, I did."

"To think that it openly encourages child abuse – it's disgusting!"

"Encourages child abuse – *The Sunday Times?* You must be joking."

"I wish I were, I wish I were."

"So how are they doing this, exactly?"

"They used to have this health-advice section, apparently."

"Oh yes, yes, I remember: in the *Style* section."

"Exactly; I've found a copy in your archives. People would write letters asking for advice, and this expert would advise them."

"I do remember; so?"

"So one piece of advice went like this."

Zinc has been linked to delayed growth, so give your children 5mg a day each.

"Hmm, I don't actually know all that much about zinc, to be honest. Perhaps the children were suffering from gigantism ..."

"Gigantism?"

"You know, when people produce too much growth hormone and grow too tall."

"No, no, *no* – this letter was from a short Malaysian lady whose children were, apparently, *below* average height. Anyway, that's what she wrote."

"O-o-o-o, I s-e-e-e-e, ha, ha, ha!"

"What's so funny?"

"Well, they must have meant the exact opposite, mustn't they?"

"The Sunday Times?"

"Yep, what they *must* have been trying to say is this."

Zinc has been linked to *promoting [OR enhancing]* growth, so give your children 5mg a day each.

"A-a-a-a ..."

"They could also have phrased it like this."

Zinc deficiency has been linked to delayed growth, so give your children 5mg of zinc a day each.

"If you're sure ..."

"Positive."

"Thank goodness for that."

"But saying the exact opposite of what you are trying to say is not all that uncommon."

"It isn't?"

"Nope. Take this, for example. From *The Economist.*"

Fewer people with less disposable income is bad news for shopkeepers.

"Isn't it?"

"No, of course not: it's *good* news for shopkeepers."

"Why?"

"Because if *fewer* people have less disposable income, then *more* people will have *more* disposable income, won't they?"

"Hmm ..."

"Hmm nothing! Look, what they must have meant was this."

Fewer people *and* less disposable income is bad news for shopkeepers.

"Are you sure?"

"Well, it can hardly be anything else. Actually, there is a pattern to such illogical reasoning."

"There is?"

"Yep; I've found this in *The Sunday Times.*"

Buying fewer clothes that are easy to wash could cut your emissions down.

"Couldn't it?"

"No, no: what would help would be buying *more* clothes that are easy to wash – *not fewer*. But they could also have meant this."

Buying fewer clothes, *and only those that are easy to wash,* could cut your emissions down.

"I s-e-e-e ..."
"And that's what they wrote in *The Independent.*"

Losses are very important to the small grower.

"Grower of what?"
"It doesn't matter of *what* – of anything that makes you money. The point is that they meant the exact opposite."
"What do you mean?"
"What do you *think* I mean? This!"

Preventing losses is very important to the small grower.

"Oh dear!"
"Exactly. And, a few days ago, that's what I heard on BBC News."

We don't want mis-selling mortgages to the wrong people.

"You mean they reckon it's OK to mis-sell mortgages to the *right* people?"
"By Jove, you got it! What this financial expert was undoubtedly attempting to say was this."

We don't want *selling* mortgages to the wrong people.

"That's more like it. But you could say it more simply – surely."
"Like what?"
"Like this."

We don't want *mis-selling mortgages.*

"Abso-bloody-lutely!
"Blimey, they don't half get muddled."
"Don't they just?"

23

An artistic journey: *The Girl with a Pearl Earring*

by Christine Mitchell

When I retired, I joined a local oil painting group tutored by Philip Macleod Coupe. I had no formal education in art, in fact not much knowledge of it altogether. The group was quite large, and we mostly painted whatever we fancied, though a still life was always set up for us.

Philip went round the group, giving hints and ideas about how to achieve the best results and occasionally giving a demonstration. He also provided books which he thought might help with our compositions. Initially, I was given instruction on what colours and brushes to acquire and on how to mix the paint. Then I completed my first, primitive, efforts.

Philip suggested that, in order to learn more about technique and composition, I should copy some paintings. I started with a Sergeant and a Sisley. The process took a lot of concentration, but the results were encouraging. I carried on with various landscapes and, when we had a sitter, an occasional portrait. I also began to collect and to study art books. I was in awe of the beauty, the technical detail and colour, particularly of the work of the Impressionists and the Old Masters, and, inspired by Philip's earlier suggestion of copying in order to improve, I decided to try to paint one of the Old Masters myself. Why not? This was the way the Royal Society of Art used to teach its students in the nineteenth century – it may still do so. The first one I chose was *The Girl with a Pearl Earring* by Vermeer.

Philip arranged for me to have a good photocopy and I picked out a canvas which was roughly the same shape as the picture I had chosen. I was lucky with *The Girl with a Pearl Earring,* as it was a small painting – about the same size as a standard modern canvas board. (Later, when copying other paintings, I had to compromise. Some of the originals were huge, the size of a wall, so I scaled them down while keeping the basic shape.)

I started with a quick sketch – not a tracing. The first part of any painting is to fill in the shapes and outlines of the composition. I enjoy the beginning, as you seem to achieve a lot in a short time, with the lights and darks contrasting and the shadow of a painting appearing. After a week, the paint has dried enough, so you can go on to stage two. Usually, when I examine what I have achieved so far and compare it to the painting, I find that the contrasts are not strong enough. Quite often, an Old Master can look very dark, but the more you look, the more you see subtle changes in colour and light. With *The Girl with a Pearl Earring,* there were also the shapes in the folds of the cloak and the turban to consider, the angle of the head, the half-frightened look in the girl's eyes and the moist half-open lips.

The background needed darkening first to highlight the subject of the painting. Next, I made my first attempt on the cloak and turban and altered the shape of her head. End of week two.

The next few weeks were spent in perfecting the clothing, the colours, the contrasts and the angles of the sitter. This took a great deal of patience. Of course, the beauty of oil paint is that you can scrape it back with a palette knife and apply more paint to change the picture. Even the Old Masters did this, as the x-rays of their paintings have shown.

Beyond the Misty Fells

Finally came the most difficult part, the face and expression. This took many weeks to perfect to Philip's and my satisfaction. The concentration needed to be intense. A small touch of white paint could complete or spoil the look of the eyes, their shape and expression. The lips were the same, as was the shadow on her neck, which pointed to her cream collar and the highlight of the pearl earring itself. Each angle and shape had to be right so that the viewer's eye was led from the eyes to the face to her unusual clothes and back again to the pearl dropping from her ear.

It took weeks of painstaking work to achieve the final result, but I was very happy with it. I have learned so much from studying the painting of an Old Master in such detail. I am not a professional artist, but, thanks to Philip's help and my own perseverance, I think I have managed to produce a successful interpretation of a magnificent work of art.

Girl with a Pearl Earring

24

Kaldi, coffee, Choche and Keswick: A journey from myth to the edge of modernity

by John Howell

Kaldi the goatherd was surprised to see several of his goats gambolling about – rather like young lambs. He had brought them to a new pasture up a hill near his village. The village was small and poor, but he had managed to raise about 15 goats through diligently seeking out ever better pastures. The goats were healthy and reaching a good weight. He was sure they would make him some money, or enable a profitable exchange, at the forthcoming Timket festival. This was the time of Christ's Epiphany and the holiest day in his church's calendar. It occurred on the 11th day of the fifth month of the Ethiopian orthodox calendar, still untouched by the ideas of Pope Gregory.

Keta Muduga, the hill where the goats were grazing, was covered in unusual bushes. They carried red berries, which seemed of great interest to these, now surprisingly lively, goats. Intrigued, Kaldi tasted a couple of berries, albeit tentatively. They had a thick red flesh with a fairly large kernel, or bean, inside. He chewed hard and found that the berries had a bland, yet slightly bitter, flavour. Later, he found himself less tired than he had expected. He did not jump about like the goats but felt invigorated and eager to get on with his work rather than just sitting idly in the grass.

After church on Sunday, he told the priest about the goats, mentioning that he had tried the berries and found that they had made him alert and eager to work. The priest was angry. He berated Kaldi for daring to seek answers outside the church. Kaldi pulled some of the berries from his pocket, and the priest grabbed them and, in his anger, threw them into the fire. Kaldi was overcome with embarrassment, but then they both noticed how wonderful the aroma given off by these burning beans was, dark and musky. Later, when Kaldi had gone, the priest took some of the charred beans from the edge of the fire and put them into the water he was carrying. He took a sip – only to find later that he had no trouble staying awake at the midnight service. Soon, all the monks were using this brew to keep awake for the night offices. The fame of the berries slowly spread from the small region of Kafa, where Kaldi lived, to the core of the empire of the legendary Queen Arwa. Today, it is Yemen, but, a thousand years ago, the countries which are now Ethiopia and Yemen were united under a single queen.

Kaldi's village of Choche, where the Arabica coffee berries had been discovered, found that coffee bushes abounded in the region. The region's farmers realised that they could trade the beans, and, over time, such trade became established. The beans were named either after Kafa or after the broader Arabian region.

The villagers could trade the beans, but the crops were small, and, even though the beans were highly prized in the towns, the profit was always creamed off by the traders and other middlemen. The bushes cropped only once a year, with the crops being very poor in alternate years. Initial prosperity turned into poverty, as the villagers always spent their coffee money long before the next harvest. Sometimes they were wealthy, sometimes poor – often over the course of a single year. The widely planted bushes got older, and, after many years, the yields slowly diminished, with new bushes being planted under shade trees only if the old tree died.

Centuries passed and modern ideas came to their country, but, for the villagers, change unfolded slowly. Life began to improve after a man called Tadesse Meskela came to the village and persuaded the farmers to form a cooperative and sell their coffee to him. They did this, and he took most of their best coffee to Addis Ababa, where he could satisfy international coffee buyers' needs for a steady supply. To develop an export market, he needed to amass coffee from several such cooperatives. Choche became more prosperous, but then, in 2002, coffee prices tumbled worldwide. Their market having turned sour, the villagers had difficulty adjusting to a lower income, tending to run out of money part-way through the year and having to rely on borrowing at high interest. Their cooperative's expenses were not covered, and it also ran up a debt, which they could not imagine repaying. Many of the farmers were near starvation.

Fortunately, the village had strong leadership, and, encouraged by Tadesse, the villagers discovered they could get a guaranteed price for their coffee if they sold it to the Fairtrade market. A further benefit of the Fairtrade system is that a premium is paid to the community in addition to the money paid to individual farmers. However, Fairtrade certification required a restructuring of the cooperative's management. First, they had to set up a democratic committee with women on the board and agree to learn how to progressively improve their crop. They were also eager to continue their organic cultivation practices and managed to get their crops certified as organic. This improved their access to markets and helped them to keep costs low. Ten years ago, the farmers were still very poor as a result of the 2001–2002 collapse in world prices, but they were well organised into a 700-strong cooperative. The cooperative would buy their crop and sell it to Tadesse's Coffee Cooperative Union. Tadesse processed the coffee at the government plant in Addis, whence it was distributed throughout the world.

Then, a group of Fairtrade campaigners from Keswick asked Tadesse to help them to find a Fairtrade-certified cooperative in the Kafa area with which they could form a link. Their goal was to highlight to fellow Keswickians the benefits of Fairtrade to the farmers in Ethiopia. Several visits to Choche were made, and three villagers visited Keswick. The visitors to Choche were shocked by how poor most of the farmers were. Their plots, extending from two to maybe 50 acres, were scarcely bigger than a country garden; most were less than 20 acres. That's where the farmers grew not only coffee for export but also, for their own subsistence, maize, teff, enset (a perennial root crop), fruits such as avocados, bananas and oranges and green vegetables. In the centre of the village, market traders displayed their meagre goods on a cloth laid on the ground. Some villagers kept bees, either in traditional cylindrical hives hung in the trees or in the more conventional rectangular hives in a corner of their gardens. Coffee honey has a rich taste and is often served to guests with freshly baked corn bread.

The visitors noticed that there were some new classrooms at the crowded primary school and were told that they had been financed with the money made on the sale of coffee to the Fairtrade market by the cooperative. This money also helped to improve some springs which were used as a water supply for both cattle and villagers: a concrete box and elevated discharge pipe would protect the water the villagers used from contamination by cattle. It was becoming clear how important Fairtrade was to the community, as Hada Biyaa, one of the women running the cooperative's committee, commented: "Fairtrade has brought us back from the dead". However, not all the farmers were members of the cooperative. Those who weren't sold to a different market, private traders – initially for a higher price, but, as a consequence, did not get the cooperative dividend later in the year. They did not, therefore, contribute to increasing the community benefits derived from the Fairtrade premium.

Some of the farmers would run out of money mid-way through the year and would thus have to mortgage their coffee crop early to private traders to get some cash to tide them over their hungry period before the next harvest. Whoever sold their coffee still in flower got only half its harvest value – an effective 100% interest on a loan for half a year. The community also suffered from unreliable water supplies, with most of the water coming from a seasonal spring, which intermittently supplied only a few standpipes sparsely distributed round the centre of a widely scattered village. Long queues of plastic water bottles would form at all the standpipes, waiting for the supply to be switched on. The school was higher up a hill and had water for only five months of the year. It taught up to grade nine only, and high school was available to just the few children who could afford weekly boarding in the nearby town of Agaro, 10 kilometres away. It was too far to walk back and forth each day. In a country which was beginning to boom, the village was falling behind.

Over recent years, Choche has embarked on a journey of gradual development. The government built a health clinic, which is larger than the one funded earlier with the Fairtrade money. The administration also sank a new well to supply water reliably all year round.

When Tadesse Meskela was visiting Fairtrade campaigners in Keswick, he mentioned the ongoing debt problem in Choche and was overheard by a local Rotarian, who realised that the Rotary organisation could set up a micro-loan scheme for the village. Rotarians from Jima near Choche and from Keswick hatched a plan and raised funds to provide Choche with a savings and loan facility. The scheme would allow small coffee farmers to avoid having to sell their 'flowers' by enabling them to borrow enough money to tide them over until the next harvest and to control their cash flow by using savings. Although the scheme was modest, it started to change the habits of many of the farmers and women. The scheme also encouraged women to borrow small start-up funds, enabling them to fatten sheep, keep hens, refine honey for market or open a shop.

The remarkable feature of the initiative was that the loans would be cross-guaranteed by the villages themselves. One year when the coffee harvest had been poor, and the time came to pay back the loans, shortfalls by some borrowers were covered by the savings of others. The loans were thus always fully repaid. The villages preserved their reputation with the Rotarians and were able to borrow again, making more profit in a good year and controlling their cash flow. They began to believe that their lives could change.

A much bigger change came about when the government's agricultural cooperative office in nearby Agaro assigned to the local villages, or kebeles, specialists who were expected to train the farmers in the use of more modern cultivation techniques and how to use compost and plant new higher-yielding coffee varieties. There was a great shortage of high-yield seedlings, so some of the women entrepreneurs set about planting seeds and growing thousands of seedlings. Once planted, seedlings would not produce a crop for three years. Making the change to new varieties would have to be done gradually, and still the farmers would need support to cover the loss of income.

Once again, the Rotary Clubs stepped in, this time mobilising a lot more money. They also asked the villagers about their priorities so that suitable plans could be made to support these. The priorities identified by the villagers were: help for the old, the widows and the orphans; help with planting the new high-yield varieties of coffee; help for women with starting and expanding small businesses; help for unemployed youths with getting a start in coffee farming. Support was also needed by groups of women who wanted to start slightly larger businesses. The Rotary Club of Keswick organised an appeal, and, with a lot of help from the Keswick and District Fairtrade campaign and other Rotary Clubs in Cumbria, enough funds were raised, over £40,000 (which came to over 1.2 million Ethiopian Birr), to start 'The Million Birr Project'. The money was used to train the farmers in modern cultivation methods and taught both women entrepreneurs and farmers how to manage their finances. In addition, about thirty young men who had never had paid work were trained and then given loans to enable them to grow high-yield coffee seedlings and fatten oxen. Women were helped with the running of their businesses, and the farmers could start planting many bushes of the new variety.

The villagers grew in confidence, some women's businesses flourished, and a savings culture spread through the community. In 2013, miraculously, the cooperative also cleared its massive 10-year-old overdraft.

There are now some further changes afoot. Affected by rapid developments in communications, electronics and transport, Ethiopia is changing rapidly. Mobile phones are cheap and already in use by many villagers. The road access, which is currently poor, will surely improve, with uncertain consequences for Choche. Global warming is spreading malaria to higher altitudes, and the disease has already reached Choche, but a widening use of bed-nets keeps it in check. The large modern university in Jimma is building a satellite campus near Agaro, and its many students will create a market for small businesses in the villages closer to the main road than Choche. Owing to climate change, coffee diseases such as the coffee bean borer are spreading up the mountains. The drive to modernisation may increase the number of large coffee plantations, displacing the smaller farmers, whose crop quality is currently superior. How will this small community adapt? Will it be able to thrive as changes fan out from the capital, or will Choche shrink back? Can Choche exploit the tourist potential of the mythical Kaldi? The journey of Choche will continue to be challenging. Hada Biyaa cryptically asked her visitors from Keswick, "Will you be with us to the end?"